Hell Yes I'm Tough Enough

By Ben Alderton

We build an election campaign to create a democracy, the campaign itself is not democratic.

Published by Playdead Press 2019

A CIP catalogue record for this book is available from the British Library.

ISBN 978-1-910067-78-9

Playdead Press
www.playdeadpress.com

Hell Yes I'm Tough Enough

By Ben Alderton

The world premiere was first performed at Park Theatre on 24th April 2019 produced by Fragen Theatre with the following cast and creative team:

CAST

Ned Contraband	**Ben Hood**
Will	**Michael Edwards**
Sharon Slaughter	**Cassandra Hercules**
Corbz	**Edward Halsted**
Poppy	**Venice Van Someren**
Patrick	**Mikhail Sen**
Glyniss	**Annie Tyson**
Nick Clog	**James Bryant**
David Carter	**Ben Alderton**

CREATIVES

Writer	**Ben Alderton**
Director	**Roland Reynolds**
Designer	**Isabella Van Braeckel**
Lighting Designer	**Alex Hopkins**
Sound Designer	**Julian Starr**
Composer	**Lewis Daniel**
Producer	**Annie Tayler**
Photography	**Robert Workman**
Public Relations	**Nick Pearce for Target Live**
Stage Manager	**Helen Thomas**
Assistant Stage Manager	**Diana Fraser**
Assistant Director	**Mariella Hudson**
Art Work	**Nathan Brenville**

With thanks to:

Nigel Wray, Saracens, Mike Haliwell, Vladimir Mirodan, Bill Britten, Moseley Ashfield CC, Shruti Haasan, Mark Duffield, Captain Morgan, Paul Goodwin, Nigel and Victoria, Matchstick Theatre, Chris Laine, Rebecca Cuthbertson, Michael Friederich, Sammy Blythe, PCT, Elena Voce and Saskia Hefes, Matthew Well-hard, Tim Klotz, Gavi Singh Chera, Aoife Smyth, Simon Dormandy, Steven Tromans, Jonathan Martin, Mia Riley, Sam West, Peter Farquhar and to all those who generously supported the fundraiser.

With special thanks to:

Old Millhillians Club, Michael Corsale, Mark Strong, Tim Corbett, Derrick Bingham, David Proudlock, Jean Stewart, Andy Johnson, John Beschizza, Dave Burnett, Will Palmer, Izaak Joel, Josh Hill, Dolly Alderton, Susan Levey, Tim Robbins, Danny Dingsdale, Park Theatre, Melli Marie, Tony and Babz, The Black Pearl, Anwar Houghton, Dr Pigeon King, Nakay Kpaka, Emma Seagull, Hannah Good, G50, the Cast and Creative teams.

And to Roly, who makes me achieve my dreams. Without his support and friendship, I would never have got here.

Ben Hood | Ned Contraband

Trained at The Univerity of Salford before training in physical theatre with Physical Lab in London.

Theatre includes: *Siren* (Matchstick Piehouse), *Fear & Loathing In Las Vegas* (The Pleasance Islington), *Antigone* (Unity Theatre Liverpool), *Cats* (The Arcola), *Dead At Last, At Last No More Air* (Camden People's Theatre), *Faulty Towers The Dining Experience, The Wedding Reception, The Grand Journey* (International Tour), *RANK* (The Lowry Theatre Salford), *The Bench* (Manchester Dance House / Library Theatre), *A bullet Through You* (The Courtyard Theatre).

Television includes: *Doctors* (BBC), *Crimewatch* (BBC).

Voice includes: *Radio 4 Afternoon Plays* (BBC), *BroBots* (Samsung VR Platforms), *Bombay Sapphire* (Online Commercial).

Film includes: *Greasy Spoon short* (Blind Aura), *Drake Feature* (Azi Rahman), *Play Judas Feature* (Red Dog Films).

Michael Edwards | Will

Trained at Drama Centre London.

Theatre includes: *Counting Sheep* (Vaults Festival), *Closer* (Vienna English Theatre), *The Fifth Column* (Southwark Playhouse), *Bruises* (Tabard Theatre), *The Emperor Self, The Dog the Night and the Knife* (Arcola Theatre), *The County* (Camden Peoples Theatre), *A Hard Rain* (Above the Stag), *Flight* (Brockley Jack), *Jekyll and Hyde* (Hong Kong Academy of Performing Arts and Southwark Playhouse), *House of Bones, The Last Days of Judas Iscariot* (Platform Theatre), *Michael Jackson at the Gates of Heaven and Hell* (Underbelly), *The Rime of the Modern Mariner* (The Dalston Old Boys Club).

Film Includes: *Uther* (Northlight Film), *1921* (Loneranger Productions), *We Don't Know Either* (Guerrero Productions), *Nearly Always* (RCA), *Fifty Eight* (YOCF), *Welcome to*

Nightvale (Redon Productions), *L'eau* (Nomentum Productions), *Tiger House* (Strike Films), *Denousa* (Venetsano Films).

Cassandra Hercules | Sharon Slaughter

Cassandra received MA Acting Degree at Guildford School of Acting in 2015. Prior to this she read Law at the Glasgow University School of Law and worked as an immigration and human rights lawyer.

Theatre includes: *One Hundred Trillion*, (Southwark Playhouse), *Lest We Forget*, (Greenwich Theatre), *The Incident* (Canada Water Theatre, Polar Union Theatre), *A Midsummer Night's Dream, The Tempest* (UK Tour), *Voices In The Dark* (Greenwich Theatre), *Inside Pussy Riot* (Saatchi Gallery), *Under My Thumb* (Edinburgh Fringe Festival, Greenwich Theatre, New Diorama Theatre), *#CASTE* (Arcola Theatre), *28 Days Later* (Secret Cinema), *Totally.*

Together (Site Specific), *Hannah and Hanna* (New Diorama Theatre, Assembly Edinburgh Fringe, Greenwich Theatre).

Film & Television includes: *Confirmation, Wolf Cry* (Music Video), *Darren Has A Breakdown* (Web Series), *Spa Brand Spot* (E4 TV Commercial), *Amanda* (Short Film), *A Mug's Game* (Feature Film) and *Do You Know Your Roots?* (MTA Productions).

Edward Halsted | Corbz

Theatre includes: *A Christmas Carol* (Windsor Castle), *People Who Need People* (Vaults Festival), *I Have Been Here Before* (Jermyn Street Theatre), *Twelve Angry Men* (National Tour), *Lady Anna: Lost at Sea* (Park Theatre & Tour), *Firebird Ball* (Punchdrunk), *The Drowned Man, Faust* (Punchdrunk / National Theatre), *Crash of the Elysium* (Punchdrunk / MIF), *The Yellow Wallpapaper* (Punchdrunk / BAC), *A Christmas*

Carol (Petersham Playhouse), *Hamlet* (GSC), *The Post Office* (British Library), *Cling to Me Like Ivy* (Birmingham Rep), *A Little Neck* (Hampton Court Palace), *Macbeth* (Big Stage Productions), *Aladdin* (Marlowe Theatre), *Josephine* (Oldham Coliseum & Tour), *Sisters And Others* (Scarlet Theatre), *Dreams Of Anne Frank* (Polka Theatre), *Single Spies* (National Theatre & West End), *Death Of A Salesman* (Nottingham Playhouse), *Gloo Joo* (Hampstead / Criterion Theatres), *Shadowlands* (Carnival Theatre), *Sherlock's Last Case, Rose, Who's Life is it Anyway?, Babes in the Wood* (Salisbury Playhouse), *Macbeth, Merchant Of Venice* (St George's), *Outside Edge* (Plymouth Theatre Royal), *Dreyfus* (Hampstead Theatre), *Phantom Of The Opera, the Bacchae* (Actors' Company), *King Lear* (Cork Opera House), *Action Replay* (Orange Tree Theatre), *James Joyce And The Israelites* (Lyric Hammersmith), *Someone Who'll Watch Over Me* (Dukes, Lancaster & Diorama), *The Tribades* (Hampstead Theatre), *Marriage Of Mr Mississippi* (New End Theatre), *Little Eyolf* (Bird's Nest), *Beat The Air* (Finborough Theatre), *Dick Whittington, Sleeping Beauty* (Windsor), *Next Time I'll Sing To You* (Millstream), *Julius Caesar, London Assurance* (Belgrade Theatre), *Gaslight, How the Other Half Loves, There's a Girl in my Soup* (Channel Theatre) and *Simon At Midnight* (Young Vic).
Television includes: *Holby City, MI High, Not Going Out, The Bill, Jonathan Creek, Kavanagh QC, Brookside, The Nation's Health, Brothers and Sisters, The Bill, Boot Street Band, 99-1, Van Der Valk, A Very British Coup, Vicar Of Dibley, Picking Up The Pieces, Fish, House Of Eliott* and *Gloo Joo.*
Film includes: *The Courier, Kinch and the Double World, Dimensions, Microscope, A Gun for George, The Magician, Clive Hole, The Misanthrope, Leon The Pig Farmer, Dinner In Purgatory, Sam-Il* and *Soho Sunset.*

Radio includes: *Whitechapel Dreams, Like They've Never Been Gone* (four series), *Church Ladies, Up Against It* and *Shadowlands.*

Venice Van Someren | Poppy
Trained at Drama Centre and École Jacques Lecoq.
Theatre includes: *The Real Thing* (Theatre Royal Bath / UK Tour), *Gabriel* (UK Tour), *Dear Brutus, Thérèse Raquin* (Southwark Playhouse), *Swallows & Amazons* (Creation) and *Can't Stand Up For Falling Down* (Theatre N16).
Film includes: *Nymphs* (Clamour), *The Girl In The Shed* (Talkies), *Silver* (BFI) and *Rites of Penance* (Raindance).

Mikhail Sen | Patrick
Trained at Drama Centre, London and The Boris Shchukin Theatre Institute, Moscow.
Theatre includes: *Troilus and Cressida* (RSC), *Taj Express* (US Tour & Sadler's Wells), *Four Play* (Muscat, Oman) and *Blood* (Royal Court).
Film includes: *3 Sleeps* (FatLip Films).
As a facilitator, he has conducted workshops for corporates, teachers and young people. He has also taught theatre at different colleges and schools in Bangalore and New Delhi.

Annie Tyson | Glyniss
Trained at Drama Centre London.
Theatre includes: *King Lear* (Old Vic), *The Enemies Within* (Young Vic), *The Seagull* (Duke of York's), *A Streetcar Named Desire, Love On The Dole* (Octagon Theatre Bolton), *The Enemies Within; The Lizzie Plays* (RADA Festival 2017), *An Honourable Man* (White Bear Theatre), *The Last Yankee* (Bolton Library Theatre).

Television includes: *How Much Is Too Much? Juliet Bravo, Casualty, Coronation Street, The Fourth Floor, King and Castle, Brookside, Damon and Debbie, A Touch of Frost* and *40*.
Film includes: *Prison Boy*.

James Bryan | Nick Clog
Trained with Fourth Monkey Theatre Company and The Actors Class, appearing in there 2017 industry showcase. James continues to program work with Theatre Deli.
Theatre includes: *Street Magic* (Bunker Theatre), *Captcha* (UK Tour).
Film includes: *PINKY*.

Ben Alderton | David Carter & Writer
Trained at Drama Centre.
Theatre includes: *You're a Good Man Charlie Brown* (Junction), *Planter's Island* (Black Box), *Mother Courage and Her Children* (Platform), *Eigengrau* (TT), *Blush of Dogs* (Tabard Theatre), *Empire Strikes Back, Dr.Strangelove, 28 Days Later* (Secret Cinema), *Faulty Towers* (ITI), *Priceless* (Matchstick).
Film includes: *Blushes* (FTN), *The Illustrious Client* (Shanghai Film Festival), *Anna Island* (LBP), *RECOIL* (Bartle Productions), *Cold Blow Lane* (LNB), *Clown Song* (Fragen Network).
Writing credits includes: *The Virgin Chronicles* (Platform Theatre), *Scandalous* (The Rag Factory), *The Strange Case Of Dr Jekyll and Mr Hyde, Dark Skies* (Platform Theatre), *Hell Yes I'm Tough Enough* (Park Theatre).

Roland Reynolds | Director
Roland Reynolds is a producer, writer and director of film, theatre and television and Artistic Director of the Fragen Network. He directed two of his own plays at the Edinburgh

Fringe Festival *Stalemate* (2008) and *Man Pursued* (2009), both produced by Richard Demarco. Since graduating from Drama Centre London in 2014, he has directed three more of his plays, *Planter's Island, Blush of Dogs* and *5 out of 10 men* as well as an original feature film, *Clown Song*, to be released in 2019.

Isabella Van Braeckel | Designer

Trained at Central St Martins.

She is a Jerwood Young Designer and Creative Associate of Fragen Theatre, Crouch End Festival Chorus and Wayward Thread Dance Arts.

Theatre includes: *Burgerz* (Mentored by Soutra Gilmour, Hackney Showroom, Manchester Royal Exchange & Tour), *Bye Bye Birdie, Our House, Candy Cansino Checks In* (Italia Conti Academy), *Finishing The Picture, Into The Numbers, A Funny Thing Happened...* (Finborough Theatre), *Midnight Train to Marrakech* (Teateri Theatre, Sweden), *Macbeth* (UK & Ireland Tour), *Othello, Two Gentlemen, Billy's Friend* (White Horse, Germany Tour), *A Midsummer Night's Dream* (The Rose Playhouse, Bankside), *Much Ado About Nothing* (RSC Dell, London), *Hamlet* (UK & Ireland Tour), *Around the World on Christmas Day, The Little Match Girl / The Fir Tree, Mirth, Marvel & Maud, 5 Out of 10 Men* (Edinburgh Fringe), *An Opera From The East* (Platform Theatre), *The Promise* (White Bear Theatre, Kings Arms Manchester), *Blush of Dogs* (Tabard Theatre), *Low Level Panic* (Etcetera Theatre), *This is Living* (Edinburgh Fringe, Theatre 503, Platform Theatre).

Film includes: *Paperboy* (Lab 91), *Kitchen Sink* (Channel 4 Random Acts 2017), *Ms Nature*, (Liam Francis), *Pray Now* (Winward Group), *Then & Now* (Camelot Films).

Opera includes: *The Travelling Companion* (New Sussex Opera, Tour), *Lansky: The Mob's Money Man*, (Crouch End Festival

Chorus, Cadogan Hall), *Die Walküre* (Grange Park Opera), *Madame Butterfly* (Cadogan Hall), *Orpheus and Eurydice* (Platform Theatre).

Dance includes: *INK* (Leicester Curve), *Finding Words* (Wayward Thread, Sadlers Wells Theatre, The Place), *Seasons* (Gors Theatre, Latvia), *Race Tracks* (Foreign Bodies Orchestra, The Place, Shambala Festival, Leicester Curve)

Events & Comedy includes: *Bec Hill: I'll be Bec* (Soho Theatre), *Paul Duncan McGarrity, A Practical Guide to Attacking Castles* (Espionage, Edinburgh Fringe), *An Audience With the Goodies* (Leicester Square Theatre).

As Associate Designer: *The Boys in the Band* (Park Theatre, UK Tour & West End).

As Assistant Designer: *Treasure* (Finborough Theatre), *Eclipsed* (Gate Theatre, Jerwood Young Designer 2015).

Design apprentice at Punchdrunk's *The Drowned Man* and *The Trench* (UK Tour, Les Enfants Terribles).

As Costume Supervisor: *Losing Venice* (Orange Tree Theatre), *Everybody's Talking About Conti* (Rhoda McGaw Theatre), *Balm in Gilead, Love & Information, Artaud at Rodez* (Platform Theatre).

Alex Hopkins | Lighting Designer

Trained at Central School of Speech and Drama.

Theatre includes: *Breathing Corpses* (Drama Centre), *A Little Warehouse* (London & Edinburgh Fringe Festival, *Thirsty* (Edinburgh Fringe Festival), *Iconic a Breath History of Drag* (UK tour) and *Oliveira's travels* (Birmingham MAC).

Julian Starr | Sound Designer

Trained at the Australian National Institute of Dramatic Arts.

Theatre includes: *Zog* (UK Tour), *Othello* (Union Theatre), *Cry Havoc* (Park Theatre), *Violet* (UK Tour), *Aisha* (Offie

Nomination Best Sound Design, London Tour), *The Orchestra* (Omnibus Theatre), *Alice In Slasherland, The Shadow Box, Telescope* (Old Fitz Theatre, Sydney), *White Noise* (Vaults Festival), *The Boy Under The Christmas Tree* (Kings Head Theatre), *Tiger Under My Skin* (Bloomsbury Theatre), *The Giant Killers* (UK Tour), *A Winning Hazard* (Finborough Theatre), *Eris* (Bunker Theatre), *Gulliver Returns* (UK Tour), *You Only Live Forever* (UK Tour), *Surf Séance* (Sydney Arts Festival), *The Comedy of Errors* (UK / Czech Republic Tour), *The Shifting Heart* (Seymour Centre Sydney), *Untold* (Playhouse Theatre Sydney), *Kapow* (Kings Cross Theatre, Sydney), *Best Before* (Sydney Fringe Festival), *The Recruiting Officer* Arts Exhibition (Hyde Park Barracks Sydney).
As Design Assistant: *Mama Mia! the Musical* (Capital Theatre Sydney), *Disney's Aladdin The Musical* (Queensland QPAC), *Talk, Richard III* (Sydney Opera House), The Royal Edinburgh Military Tattoo (Edinburgh Castle).

Lewis Daniel | Composer
Lewis studied at The Brit School of Performing Arts and then the Guildhall School of Music and Drama on the Jazz course. Over the years he has performed with such artists such as Tom Grennan, Rachel Kerr, Katy B, Beverly Knight, MJ Cole, The Muppets and stared in a Virgin Internet Commercial as a musician. Currently Lewis writes and arranges the horn section for the House Gospel Choir, a choir which mixes house music with gospel music and have recently being signed to Island Records. He runs his own horn section called the Biscuit Horns which provides bespoke horn section parts and performances for artists.
Lewis is part of the Matchstick Theatre Company providing music for many of their plays and productions.

Annie Tayler | Producer

Producing credits include: *Eigengrau* (Brighton Fringe, Kings Head) which was nominated for two Off West End Awards and *My Turn Now* a new piece of writing by Ella Saltmarshe based around the book *Growing Old Disgracefully* which looks at the ways women are represented as they age. She is co-founder of campaign *RepresentAge* which is tackling the representation of women and works with theatre professionals, TV and film companies and advertising agencies to try and change the problem at its route.

Production Manager credits include: *Below The Belt* (Pleasance, Edinburgh) and *Lean* (Tristan Bates).

Annie works as Marketing and Communications Officer at Gunnersbury Park & Museum and offers freelance marketing consultation in various arts settings.

Fragen Theatre Company

Fragen Theatre Company is the theatre arm of the Fragen Network, an international collective of artists, writers and actors who produce theatre, cinema and television.

Founded in 2014, Fragen Theatre has a mission to produce new writing. Theirs is physical, political and powerful work that challenges our assumptions and cognitive biases.

They have produced such critically acclaimed shows as *Planter's Island* (2014), *Blush of Dogs* (2015) and *5 out of 10 men* (2016). *Hell Yes I'm Tough Enough* (2019) at Park Theatre will be followed by a residency at Teatr 18+'s 2019 summer festival in Rostov-on-the-Don, Russia, and new play *Fragile Matter* at the Old Red Lion (2020).

About Park Theatre

Park Theatre was founded by Artistic Director, Jez Bond and Creative Director, Melli Marie. The building opened in May 2013 and, with four West End transfers, two National Theatre transfers and ten national tours in its first five years, quickly garnered a reputation as a key player in the London theatrical scene. Park Theatre has received two Olivier nominations, won an Offie for Best New Play (*The Revlon Girl*), Best Set Design (*Distance*), Best Foodie Experience, and won The Stage's Fringe Theatre of the Year in 2015.

Park Theatre is an inviting and accessible venue, delivering work of exceptional calibre in the heart of Finsbury Park. We work with writers, directors and designers of the highest quality to present compelling, exciting and beautifully told stories across our two intimate spaces.

Our programme encompasses a broad range of work from classics to revivals with a healthy dose of new writing, producing in-house as well as working in partnership with emerging and established producers. We strive to play our part within the UK's theatre ecology by offering mentoring, support and opportunities to artists and producers within a professional theatre-making environment.

Our Creative Learning strategy seeks to widen the number and range of people who participate in theatre, and provides opportunities for those with little or no prior contact with the arts.

In everything we do we aim to be warm and inclusive; a safe, welcoming and wonderful space in which to work, create and visit.

★★★★★ "*A five-star neighbourhood theatre.*" Independent

As a registered charity [number 1137223] with no public subsidy, we rely on the kind support of our donors and volunteers. To find out how you can get involved visit **parktheatre.co.uk**

For Park Theatre

Artistic Director | Jez Bond
Executive Director | Rachael Williams
Associate Artistic Director | Melli Marie
Development Director | Dorcas Morgan
Sales & Marketing Director | Dawn James
Sales & Marketing Manager | Rachel McCall
Finance Manager | Elaine Lavelle
Finance & Administration Officer | Susie Italiano
Development & Production Assistant | Daniel Cooper
Technical & Buildings Manager | Sacha Queiroz
Deputy Technical & Buildings Manager | Neal Gray
Administrator | Melissa Bonnelame
Community Engagement Manager | Nina Graveney-Edwards
Access Coordinator | Sarah Howard
Venue & Volunteer Manager | Barry Card
Duty Venue Managers | Abigail Acons-Grocock, Natasha Green, Shaun Joynson, Michael Peavoy
Head of Food & Beverage | Brett Reynolds
Food and Beverage Senior Supervisor | Oli Mortimer
Café Bar Team | Grace Boateng, Robert Czibi, Gemma Barnet, Josh Oakes Rodgers, Amy Conway, Matt Littleson, Ryan Peek, Alice Pegram, Ewan Brand, Adam Harding Kheir, Sebastian Harker, Jack Mosedale, Maisie Saidgrove, Florence Blackmore, Kerry Hunt, James Bradwell, Yan Tobi Amisi
Senior Box Office Supervisor | Natasha Green
Box Office Supervisors | Greg Barnes, Natalie Chan, Jack Mosedale
Public Relations | Nick Pearce and Julie Holman for Target Live

President | Jeremy Bond

Trustees
Andrew Cleland-Bogle
Nick Frankfort
Robert Hingley
Mars Lord
Sir Frank McLoughlin
Bharat Mehta
Rufus Olins
Nigel Pantling (Chair)
Victoria Phillips
Jo Parker

Ambassadors
David Horovitch
Celia Imrie
Sean Mathias
Tanya Moodie
Hattie Morahan
Tamzin Outhwaite
Meera Syal

Associate Artist
Mark Cameron

With thanks to all of our supporters, donors and volunteer

CHARACTERS

The Red Party

Ned Contraband
(Leader of the Red Party)

Will
(Ned's Life Coach)

Sharon Slaughter
(Media Strategist and Advisor)

Corbz
(The Wise Janitor)

The Blue Party

David Carter
(Leader of the Blue Party and Prime Minister)

Glyniss
(Campaign Manager)

Nick Clog
(Leader of the Yellow Party and Deputy Prime Minister)

Poppy
(Coffee girl)

Patrick
(Election Consultant)

This play is based on real events and extensive research. Many aspects of the dialogue and character have been devised for the purpose of dramatization and comedy.

/ indicates overlapping or intruding

... Indicates search for thought

. Indicates end of thought

Prologue

Right wing.
Left wing.
Wing Commander.
Tory.
Toff.
Sticky toffee pudding.
Liberals.
Lefties.
Liberal Democrat.
Cossack.
Syria.
Sierra Leone.
Leona Lewis.
IT ALL SEEMED LIKE YESTERDAY SO FAR AWAY.
Lewis.
Endeavour.
Morse.
Morse code.
Code breaker.
BENEDICT CUMBERBATCHY.
Masons.
Corrupt.
Mail.
Mail on Sunday.
Sunday Times.
The Times.
THE TIMES THEY ARE CHANGING.
Miley Cyrus.
Virus.
Twerk it.

Work it.
Burn it.
Harder.
Faster.
Stronger.
Are you beach body ready?
Thighs.
Fat.
Trans fat.
Transgender.
Transformers.
The robots are in disguise.
Virus.
Hacking.
Haddock.
Salmon.
Divide.
Independence.
Ridiculous.
SNP.
BBC.
BNP won't you dance with me?
Blue.
Red.
Yellow.
Black.
White.
Brown.
Labelling.
Labelled.
Gay.
Straight.

Islamic.
Trans.
Translamic.
Immigration.
Emigration.
Intimidation.
Intermediation.
Grey.
Beige.
Vage'.
Vagasil.
Aisle nine
Purple.
PURPLE RAIN, PURPLE RAIN.
Rock star.
Jesus.
Kanye West.
Fred West.
Prostitute.
Lady of the night.
Night crawlers.
Cucumber thief.
Crack.
Coke.
Lines.
Metropolitan.
District.
Circle.
THEY SIT ON THEIR ARSE ALL DAY AND STILL GET THIRTY K.
Special K.
Couch Potato.

Union.
TFL.
Tetley.
Tea.
Yorkshire.
Ripper.
Rotherham.
Enquiries.
7/7.
9/11.
2012.
We mustn't talk about it.
Don't talk about it.
I don't want to talk about it.
The British way.
Farmers' Market.
Eggs.
Prescott.
Heavyweight.
Lightweight.
Blair.
Promises.
Broken.
Bent.
Iraq.
Belfast.
Orange.
Green.
Recycle.
Boris bike.
Pollution.
Polls.

Jews.
Miliband.
Misunderstood.
Misrepresented.
Representation.
Proportional.
Cameron.
Tory.
Toff.
Twat.
Saviour.
Lucky.
Minority.
Majority.
Ivory Tower.
TEAR IT DOWN START AGAIN.

Act I

(*Spotlight up on Patrick standing centre stage. He means what he says*)

PATRICK: Every single person is extraordinary. The tragedy is we have a society where too many people never get to fulfil that potential. The government's job is to help them do it, not to tell people how to live their lives, but release their potential, no matter who they are. We must take power away from those who hoard it. Challenge vested interests. Break down privilege that blocks opportunity and progress. And give everyone a chance to live the life they want. The British political system is broken, it always has been. And now it's time to fix it.

(*Spotlight up on David Carter standing stage left. He is ready*)

CARTER: Yes, thank you, good question Barbara, thank you for firing that one at me. Now let me answer you directly. We will not negotiate with extremists. Absolutely not.

(*Spotlight up on Ned Contraband standing stage right. He is not ready*)

NED: No, no I don't actually; I don't think they'll execute Mr Morgan. I think they've got a terrible poker face, they're deeply insecure, terribly neglected (one might say misunderstood) quite sensitive extremists, and they can wave their large knives all they like but you're fooling no one gents.

CARTER: No Ian I do not have a stake in my father's offshore investment fund, and I think it is incredibly inappropriate to ask me those sorts of questions at a time like this

NED: Yes I do have something to say to their leader… Mr Abu Quartarder, listen… wind your neck in young man; you are so out of your depth sunshine

CARTER: Okay, what I am saying is very simple… Do I think we're at risk from a terrorist attack in London? No. Do I think we should be worried about it…? Yes. Is it going to happen? Definitely not. Could it happen in the near future? Probably, yes. Do we need to be anxious or worried? No, not in the slightest. Should we prepare ourselves for the worst…? I think that would be very wise yes

NED: What can Londoners do to prevent terrorist attacks? Very good question. Basically… nothing. If it's going to happen, it's going to happen, c'est la vie

CARTER: Look I can't be any clearer on the matter. There aren't any signs; there is nothing to look out for

NED: I mean there are a few signs you could look out for. Suspicious behaviour, secret meetings. And if you have any *awarity* that a neighbour or loved one is premeditating a terrorist attack, you should address it. You know, go up to them and say *"No. Intervention. What you're doing is bang out of order"*

CARTER: Ladies and gentlemen, I have just been informed, just now, of the tragic news that Charles Morgan has been executed. At this time I would like to express my sincere condolences and prayers to the Morgans, his wife Nora, and three boys (*Looking at the writing on his hand*) Jake, Harry and Leon. Leo, during this ghastly and deeply harrowing time

(*Silence*)

Charlie loved his family, he loved people, he loved his job. He would go above the call of duty to report news from the front beyond his position as a journalist. This is a sad day. A day of mourning, a day of reflection. A day of not pointing fingers and probing investigation

NED: (*Surprised*) Oh has he? Oh no… that's sad that is. Oh I am so very sorry… I'm cross now, I'm really am very cross about that. I cannot portray how cross I actually am

CARTER: To make it perfectly clear (in a court of law) Charles Morgan went above and beyond what he wasn't asked to do, what he was not contractually obliged to do… but as I said it's a very sad situation

NED: Well clearly the blame lies with the Prime Minister. He is the one with blood on his hands. Shame on him

CARTER: Let's not start a witch hunt shall we. A man has died under the most gruesome circumstances, we must allow the Morgans to grieve and not perverse into an investigation.

NED: He's a snake and a liar not fit to spend another term in office. If the PM had any respect for Mr Morgan and his family, he would resign, immediately

CARTER: No of course I'm not going to bloody resign

NED: No I am not overreacting. DAVID CARTER IS THE REINCARNATION OF HITLER HIMSELF!

CARTER: Contraband is clearly panicking under pressure because he knows his popularity is depressingly low. And I have it on good authority that there is a vote of "No confidence" within his party

NED: Lies, all lies

CARTER: Who is the best PM of all time? (*Smiling*) That's a tricky question… I'm gonna have to say Maggie (*Laughs*) Yes she caused huge divide within our country, leading to mass unemployment and poverty, however she was our first female PM and shaped the Britain we are living in today. Plus I have to say it was a hell of an achievement for a woman to fight such horrendous sexism in a male dominated society. For I am fully aware of the inequality that still exists for women today... which my party swears to eradicate by the way.

NED: Who is the best PM of all time? Answer. Me

CARTER: Do you really want a flaky, lightweight imbecile to run this country? Contraband is a little lost boy in a man's world

NED: I am not a boy, I am a man. A real man, a Prime Minister man!

CARTER: Am I tough enough to run this country? Come on love, I've managed to steer this nation through a quadruple dip recession. Tina, honey, you tell me? Am I tough enough?

NED: I will tell you this Barbara... A new power is rising "The Lost Prince" the chosen one. A sturdy leader ready to change this country for the greater good, and yes, I am that Prince.

CARTER: It is my mission to switch on a whole new generation and make them feel groovy about being Conservative again

NED: No longer must we live under fear, misery and austerity. No longer Phyliss do we have to endure a coalition that has betrayed us. No longer do we have to live under a parliament that doesn't actually represent the great people of Britain. Yes, a new power is rising. And I demand David Carter faces me in a televised debate so I can expose him as the slug, the mollusc that he is. Am I tough enough? Hell yes I'm tough enough!

(*Silence*)

Did you get all that?

(*Lights out*)

(*Lights up, outside Number 10. Patrick arrives on his bike. He is average height, Indian, mid 20s wearing a bike helmet and fluorescent vest. He is very invested in what he does. He carries a large briefcase and folders. He is quite nervous, it is his first day. His trousers remain tucked into his socks*)

PATRICK: (*Staring at the big black door*) Be the change you wish to see. (*Goes for the handle*)

(*Glyniss bursts out. She is barking down the phone whilst juggling a coffee holder with several beverages and documents tucked under her arms. She is in her 50s, well turned out. Very tough, quite posh*)

GLYNISS: (*On the phone*) Yes I know darling but I can't just drop everything I'm… why? Because I've got an election campaign to run you silly prick… well tell her to pull her finger out and stop all this self-indulgent malarkey… (*Shocked*) She what…? Yes, fine! I'll sort it out… Geoffrey…! I'll sort it out (*She hangs up*) Christ!

PATRICK: Bad news?

GLYNISS: (*Turning to him surprised*) inconvenient news, my daughter's been expelled doing coke lines off her hockey stick.

PATRICK: Oh… what uni is she at?

GLYNISS: She's fourteen the selfish fucking cow.

PATRICK: Right

GLYNISS: I know. Toddlers will be dealing anytime soon

PATRICK: Sorry that must be tough?

GLYNISS: Oh no I can forgive Jemima, bless her. Being daughter of the mum that works for the PM means peer pressure is the only way she can make any friends whatsoever. We've had to move school four times in the last year, occupational hazard. (*Surveys him*) You're one of the new campaign consultants aren't you?

PATRICK: Yes, hi (*Shakes her hand*) nice to meet you Mrs Sanchez

GLYNISS: Don't call me Mrs for fuck sake, makes me feel middle aged. Call me Glyniss, or Gilly after a few dry whites. And you must be…

PATRICK: Pa/

GLYNISS: No wait! Let me guess, I Wikipediad you this morning… Ahmed? Arjet? Gary? Muhammad? Bertie? Bertreum? Percy? Arjun? Leon? Larry? (Not Larry) Akshay? Kenneth? Kabir? (Stop me once I hit it) Ramesh? Phil? Patrick? Kent / Kevin?

PATRICK: You hit it!

GLYNISS: Oh did I? What... Kent? Really? That's a ridiculous name, you're not a county

PATRICK: Paddy... Patrick

GLYNISS: Irish, very sexy (*They shake hands firmly*)

PATRICK: No just unfortunate

GLYNISS: Yes, you're far too tanned to be a Celt. Terribly sorry, I literally meet a thousand nobodies a week with all these monotonous middle England names, none of them stick, menopause eh? It's a fucker... Percy?

PATRICK: Patrick

GLYNISS: Did you get the files last night?

PATRICK: Yes! Ploughed through, got the gist

GLYNISS: Great! Excellent! Right, well forget all that we've changed it entirely

PATRICK: Oh...

GLYNISS: 'Fraid so... George didn't like it, said it was Swiss cheese

PATRICK: Swiss?

GLYNISS: Too many holes

PATRICK: Right, gotcha... any key things before I dive in?

GLYNISS: All hands on deck really, we've got a campaign to win. Say so long farewell to your social life as you'll never see daylight again and live off four hours sleep for the next twenty years (That is of course if you're not sacked) Get ready for coffee carb addiction and putting on two stone just to get through this depressing occupation called politics. It's fucking great, livin' the dream. Here cupcake, take a cappuccino

PATRICK: I don't drink coffee

GLYNISS: Yes you bloody well do, won't last two hours (*She goes for the door*)

PATRICK: Sorry, before we go in, can I just say… I think you're amazing

GLYNISS: (*Stunned*) I'm sorry?

PATRICK: You were my idol at uni, I did my thesis on you. The machine behind the Tories for the last fifteen years, "Thatcher's apprentice, the real PM" the only reason the conservatives were ever in power… you're just… incredible. You are / literally

GLYNISS: Pat, munchkin. As lovely as it is for you to blow smoke up my arse, I really don't respond well to flattery. It's my job. I'm not saving lives or changing the world or being shot at; I'm just a campaign manager. Most of the time I'm just trying to get through the day without a bomb going off somewhere, declaring war on some barbaric country or crucifying our useless PM, whilst trying to keep my daughter happy and my tattered marriage together. What really keeps me going aren't the exciting new policies, ground breaking manifestos or changing this wonderful country, but having several pints of gin at the end of the week.

PATRICK: (*Shocked*) Oh right… sorry

GLYNISS: Christ you're not used to this level of cynicism are you? You consultants are so much more sensitive and civilised

PATRICK: Sorry I wasn't brown nosing, just so amazing to meet you in the flesh

GLYNISS: Darling, darling, treacle… it's fine, honestly. I'm glad you did it before stepping into No. 10; they'd have had you for breakfast. Plus, you're welcome to see me in the flesh anytime (*Winks then slaps his arse*)

PATRICK: Are there any absolute dos or don'ts?

GLYNISS: Yes. Ignore anything Nick Clog says, ever!

PATRICK: But he's the deputy PM?

GLYNISS: Yes? So? He's not important. Marianna the cleaning lady has more influence than him

PATRICK: What about Dave?

GLYNISS: For God's sake don't call him that. Sir or Prime Minister. And never refer to him as a Toff, it really pisses him off (*Going for the door*)

PATRICK: I was hoping to pitch my idea on "People's Banking", the/ cash

GLYNISS: No, no, no, absolutely not! Disgracefully bad timing, naughty boy. You haven't even stepped in the door

PATRICK: But that's why I'm here

GLYNISS: Pudding, you have to play the game, okay? David doesn't give a shit about what you have to say. He trusts no one, bar me and George Oblong. All you have to do, right now, is have cast iron bollocks and not slip under the radar

PATRICK: Be heard but not opinionated

GLYNISS: Exactly

PATRICK: Like a 50s housewife

GLYNISS: And for the love of God do not let him bully you

PATRICK: I'm sure I'll be fine

GLYNISS: No you won't, this is No. 10, it's a strip club on acid, absolute pandemonium! Really show some balls. We like that, David loves balls. Now come on ducky, in we pop.

(*They enter No. 10. We hear constant ringing, buzzing, notifications and alerts. It never stops, it's like a call centre. Civil servants on edge, coming and going in a great hurry, carrying documents. It's countdown to the General Election*)

PATRICK: Just one thing Glyniss, what about the refugee housing policy?

GLYNISS: Seriously you need to pipe the fuck down or I'll send you to the naughty corner. Play the game

PATRICK: But I'm here to advise / you

GLYNISS: No, no you're not. Everyone wants to pitch their policies. You're about to enter the asylum of the most egotistical and obnoxious men this country has to offer (*Her phone starts to buzz. She rapidly takes it out*) Jesus fuck it's the Russians (*Answers the phone*) Vladimir! Khoroshego dnya (*She flirts unapologetically*) You've been a really naughty bear haven't you… (*She giggles*) Vladimir stop it, I'm a married woman… Well stop piddling around and stoking a civil war… you haven't got many friends in Europe silly sausage so I wouldn't start making demands if I were you… well you really pissed him off… okay poppet, I'll see what I can do… yes Vlad, the flowers and chockies were very much appreciated… until our next encounter, proschai (*She hangs up, shivers*) Feel like a centipede has crawled up my vagina.

PATRICK: (*Stunned*) Was that Vladimir Pu/

GLYNISS: Not a bloody word!

(*Nick Clog enters. He is a short man, very smiley and enthusiastic. No one cares about him*)

CLOG: Gilly, Hiiiiiiiiiiiiiii. How are you love muffin? (*He kisses her cheek*)

GLYNISS: Nick don't do that otherwise I'll put you on a register.

CLOG: All right, don't flatter yourself love (*Turns to Patrick*) Hi, Nick, deputy PM

GLYNISS: Deputy to the PM

CLOG: Pat right?

PATRICK: Absolute privilege to meet you Sir

CLOG: Please… oh fantastic work in Croydon by the way; you turned that shithole right around.

PATRICK: I can't take full credit, I was just the PR guy

CLOG: Nonsense, I've read your eco war challenge and immigrant tackling policies

PATRICK: Again, just luck and timing

GLYNISS: (*Whilst on the phone*) Don't suck his cock Nick he's just the intern

CLOG: No Gilly he's "The Fixer" the guru consultant

GLYNISS: Oh darling you're the kid genius, sorry love. There was me thinking you weren't important and went to one of those shitty northern unis

PATRICK: (*He chuckles*) I did

CLOG: (*Politely*) Oh which one?

PATRICK: It really doesn't matter

GLYNISS: It does here. If you're not Oxbridge you're out the door old chap

PATRICK: Well I think we need to challenge all those generalisations and stereotypes

CLOG: Right we fucking do, I like this kid Gilly, he's got balls. We like balls

GLYNISS: (*Still on the phone*) You bloody leave him alone you

PATRICK: Actually Nick our policies really do crossover, I applied to your party but you're a tight knit bunch

CLOG: That we are my friend, Ashdown was very Masonic

PATRICK: I feel we're on the same wavelength on the EU, we can't ignore it/ much

CLOG: All in good time old sport, all in good time... baby doll, did you get my email last night?

GLYNISS: (*Still on the phone*) Yes I did you bloody sex pest. Stop waking me up at three in the morning with your silly ideas, no one cares

CLOG: (*Offended*) Right! Fine! Well how *fucking* unprofessional! I'm sure the PM will have something to say about this

GLYNISS: Nick! Don't! It will just end in tears

CLOG: Well I think you're wrong there sweetheart

(*Poppy enters. She's mid 20's, posh. The PM has hired her for one reason. Glyniss despises her*)

POPPY: Gertrude?

GLYNISS: Glyniss. What Poppy?

POPPY: Dave's just coming through now

GLYNISS: The *PM* is coming through now, he's half an hour late

POPPY: He had a meeting with the treasury

GLYNISS: Why was I not informed?

POPPY: Oh I didn't think he needed you?

GLYNISS: But he told you though?

POPPY: Yes

GLYNISS: Then why didn't you tell me?

POPPY: Does he need you?

GLYNISS: Sweetie… he *always* needs me

POPPY: Oh sorry Gladys

GLYNISS: Glyniss. Mrs Sanchez or Senior CO to you

POPPY: Senior, yes I can tell... we need to brief at 9:45 for the Danish Ambassador

GLYNISS: Yes quite right, well get everyone assembled (*Poppy goes to exit*) And Poppy

POPPY: (*Innocently*) Yes?

GLYNISS: That's a lot of makeup

POPPY: Oh is it?

GLYNISS: You know it is. This isn't a Chinese brothel, get some baby wipes and sort your life out

POPPY: Sorry Geraldine, some of us like to make an effort

(*She exits swiftly*)

GLYNISS: Fucking bimbo, I will literally knife her after the election

CLOG: Oooooo Mother Goose threatened by the younger, fertile, more succulent bird?

GLYNISS: Really, you find that attractive do you?

CLOG: Oh come on Gill she's sex on legs! Don't get me wrong you scrub up pretty well for fifty-five, but she could suck the skin off a banana!

GLYNISS: She tarts herself up and bats her eyelids just to get Dave's attention so one day he'll promote her from coffee girl to chancellor

CLOG: Yeah but have you seen that arse? Nice bit of eye candy eh? (*Nudges Patrick*)

PATRICK: This is incredibly inappropriate

CLOG: Oh come on! The talent is pretty low round here. It's just fat girls and middle aged spinsters, no offence!

(*Glyniss smacks Clog hard with a cabinet briefcase*)

PATRICK: This isn't democratic!

(*We hear David Carter arriving; he is singing an entrance song whilst dancing followed by Poppy*)

CARTER: This hit, That ice cold, Michelle Pfeiffer, That white gold, This one, for them hood girls, Them good girls, Straight masterpieces, Stylin', while in, Livin' it up in the city, Got Chucks on with Saint Laurent, Got kiss myself I'm so pretty. I'm too hot

CLOG: Hot damn, called a police and a fireman

CARTER: I'm too hot

CLOG: Hot damn, make a dragon wanna retire man

CARTER: I'm too hot

POPPY: Hot damn, say my name you know who I am

CARTER: I'm too hot

POPPY: Hot damn, am I bad 'bout that money

CARTER: Break it down

CLOG: Girls hit your hallelujah

POPPY: Whuoo!

CLOG: Girls hit your hallelujah

POPPY: Whuoo!

CLOG: Girls hit your hallelujah

POPPY: Whuoo!

CLOG: Cos uptown funk gon' give it to you

POPPY: Cos uptown funk gon' give it to you

CLOG/POPPY: Saturday night and we in the spot, don't believe me just watch!

CARTER: What fantastic song writing, who says I'm not down with current affairs? (*He starts dancing round Glyniss*)

GLYNISS: Have you been drinking?

CARTER: I've had a few fucking drinks

GLYNISS: (*Remains still*) David why didn't you inform me about the treasury?

CARTER: The what sweet cheeks?

GLYNISS: Stop. (*He does*) The treasury?

CARTER: There is nothing to tell, gotta...gotta learn to listen Gilly

GLYNISS: I should have been there. Oh and by the way... Vladimir Pubein wants you to go to Moscow

CARTER: No, he's taking the piss the filthy Cossack

GLYNISS: I'll say you're indisposed for now. We also have dinner with the Italian President/ this evening

CARTER: (*Sings in a terrible Italian accent*) When tha moon hits your eye lika big pizza pie, That's amore

CLOG: (*Falsetto*) that's amore

GLYNISS: I'm sure he'll appreciate that

CARTER: Pretty lady shutuppa your fayce! Mamma Mia, spaghetti bolognaise

GLYNISS: We *need* to be hospitable

CARTER: (*Sings*) Welcome Italia to our family

CLOG: (*Sings*) You bring us lasagne from Italy

GLYNISS: Enough! Last thing on the menu boys is we need to talk campaign strategy now. Contraband threw down the gauntlet last night with that little stunt he pulled with the whole Morgan inquiry

CARTER: No that was a special needs kid losing his shit on national television

GLYNISS: Nevertheless we need to put gears in motion, there's only ten weeks to go

CARTER: Listen the Chuckle Brothers have a better shot at running the country than he does

CLOG: I dunno Dave, there are national doubts over your appetite and motivation

(*Silence*)

CARTER: You what mate?

(*Silence. Everyone is very scared*)

Sorry did you say something Clog?

CLOG: No it's just fact… you can't argue / he's doing

CARTER: Oi ! Oi…! Calm your noise. It's 9:30 Clog. What time does that mean?

CLOG: Skinny Latte?

CARTER: Skinny Latte.

CLOG: Right you are David

CARTER: Now off you fuck you arse clown rent boy

CLOG: Sorry Dave/ I just

CARTER: Are you still here? ***(He exits swiftly)*** Bloody Liberals

GLYNISS: David we need to stick to our game plan otherwise that moron Nigel Garage will get the media's panties wet over the thought of a coalition with us and UKRAP

CARTER: Is he being genuinely serious?

GLYNISS: Deadly. He even twatted it on social media last night, look at the twat he posted

CARTER: Glyniss...what are you wearing?

GLYNISS: (*Looks at herself*) What? What do you mean?

CARTER: You're almost sixty for Christ sake, pull your skirt down

GLYNISS: David!

CARTER: What?

GLYNISS: Just! Fucking! Don't!

CARTER: Alright calm your badger, who's this tosser?

GLYNISS: Campaign consultant, he's new

CARTER: Punjab right?

PATRICK: Patrick, hello sir

GLYNISS: "The Fixer" (*Her phone rings*)

CARTER: Ohhhhhhh.......you're the guru kid the Standard won't stop tugging themselves dry over. Has the crypt keeper filled you in?

PATRICK: Yeah she's been great… I just wanted to thank you / for letting me

CARTER: You were the Croydon lad with the bright ideas about them dirty immigrants…? I am joking by the way… or am I?

PATRICK: Well, yes… I still stand firm on my article that your Conservative principles are outdated for/ modern Britain

CARTER: So go on then. What's your verdict on my campaign?

PATRICK: Seriously… How long have you got?

CARTER: Well you've got thirty seconds

PATRICK: Right, okay, wow… well essentially what you have is pretty concrete, but you lack a defining policy. You need to hone the election messages so they are ingrained in people's minds then relentlessly repeat and reinforce, making them clear and coherent. Get in early and weed out the potentially convertible voters. This will be won by cyber, air and ground war via direct mail, Twitter and Facebook. Never underestimate the power of social media. You need to stop branding yourself as this self-regurgitated Neo Conservative. You are still in essence right wing and sceptical towards radical, revolutionary ideas and you patronise your voters by saying you have shifted towards the left. You need to completely rebrand yourself, reshape and evolve your party, purging the memory of Thatcherism by building this modern, flexible, adaptable, compassionate, socially, economically and environmentally aware party, embracing new roots. Internally you need to scourge all stuffy, old-fashioned Tories and corrupt individuals, reduce your party to a more compact, hardworking, trustful army. Recruit young politicians from local boroughs and bring a fresh exciting new energy and policies. This will gain younger voters eventually with the hope of making politics sexy again and something to be emotionally and morally invested in. But most importantly you need to show the public through guts and passion that you care otherwise you *will* lose

(*Silence*)

CARTER: Well I just got into politics for the pussy and cocktails

PATRICK: (*He laughs*) I'm not sure I believe that

CARTER: Believe what you want mate, none of us are saints. It's called practicality... you wanna drink? (*He pours two very large whiskeys from a decanter*)

PATRICK: It's 9am

CARTER: And what?

PATRICK: It's just a bit unprofessional

CARTER: It'll calm your nerves. I really do insist

PATRICK: I'm fine Mr Carter, thank you

CARTER: Have a drink

(*Silence*)

PATRICK: I'm fine. Thank you

CARTER: I'm having one too

GLYNISS: (*Whilst on the phone*) What's going on, what are you doing? Patrick don't drink that

CARTER: Shut the fuck up

(*Silence*)

Go on, drink it

PATRICK: I'm really okay

CARTER: I wasn't asking

(*Silence. Patrick smiles, gives in and timidly takes the glass and sips it. David death stares him. Patrick in fear downs the rest. He coughs. David then hands him another and nods to him. Patrick hesitates, then downs the second*)

Good boy (*Going up to him*) Remember you are very lucky to be here (*Glyniss enters*)

GLYNISS: Oh for God's sake! (*She takes the glass off Patrick, then hands him a bottle of water*) Grow the fuck up David. (*To Patrick*) What did I say?

PATRICK: Yes, sorry

GLYNISS: (*Handing him some documents*) Get out now

(*Patrick shuffles off with his papers. Carter just smiles at Glyniss*)

You listen here. There is no time for this public school bollocks do you hear me? Right now you are losing to Contraband. Take the piss out of him all you like but you are staggering behind my friend without a pot to piss in

CARTER: I very much beg to differ. You forget what happens when I'm in front of a camera... we've got this in the bag baby doll

(*Clog enters with coffee mugs and hands one to Carter, he takes a glug then immediately spits the burning hot coffee into Clog's face. He falls to his knees in agony*)

(*Throws the cup on the ground*) I asked for a skinny latte you prick, this tastes of spunk!

GLYNISS: (*Firmly*) Calm down David

CLOG: (*Wiping himself down*) they had no milk so I used soya

CARTER: Well what have we learnt today Clog?

CLOG: (*Crying*) Soya tastes of spunk?

CARTER: Soya tastes of spunk. Now get out of my sight before I decapitate you. (*Clog goes to exit*) Actually no, wait, come here. (*He does*) Everyone get out here

GLYNISS: David this is unnecessary

CARTER: Shut up (*The office assembles*) This, is what happens ladies and gents when you try to fuck with the PM. Understand? I'm the Demon Headmaster in this joint, and if any fag thinks they're hard enough, I'll send them back to boarding school with their trousers down. (*He grabs Clog by the scruff of the neck*) This cock-riding pigmy tried to disrespect me…! He got it *very* wrong.

GLYNISS: It's just a skinny latte

CARTER: It's the principal you silly woman… Now if anyone else fancies playing silly buggers there's the door. I am the best, and I demand the best. I cannot stress to you how imperative it is for you, your families, your children, your pet dog, your pet turtle that we do. Not. Lose. Otherwise? End of! As you were, class dismissed… now clean my shoes

CLOG: (*Sobbing*) What?

CARTER: Clean up my fucking shoes (*Nick wipes David's shoes clean. He takes the dirty tissues and exits, Poppy enters*) Poppy, how are you?

POPPY: I'm great thanks, how are you?

CARTER: All the better for seeing you me dear

POPPY: Awww thank you Mr Carter

CARTER: Please, call me Dave (*He winks*)

POPPY: (*She giggles*) David stop it…! Well maybe I shall, big Dave

CARTER: Oooooooooooooooooo. (*He chuckles*) Oh Poppy, you are so dirty… that's a very nice skirt

POPPY: Oh what this old thing?

CARTER: And someone is looking slamming in those heels, can I ask… did it hurt?

POPPY: Did what hurt?

CARTER: Fallin' from Heaven. (*They both laugh*) You settling in okay pop star?

POPPY: Yes thank you, everyone's lovely

CARTER: We're just one big happy family here. You, being the new (disgracefully sexy) daughter; Patrick your excitable, sexually confused brother; Nick the perverted uncle we had to section; Glyniss being your great great grandmother leaving the remote control in the fridge and complaining about the Arabs. The whole place is just full of love and mutual respect. I don't want you to think of me as a boss or the man in charge of literally everything, but more as a friend

POPPY: I look forward to our ever-growing relationship Mr Prime Minister. Did you get my email by the way?

CARTER: (*In discomfort*) I did yes

POPPY: (*Excited*) And?

CARTER: (*Hesitates*) I honestly think it's a cracking idea, I really do. The only issue is (If I'm brutally honest) calling a referendum could be the biggest backlash of my career. Can we not just leave it in Parliament?

POPPY: (*Sternly*) Well that's the point, it's not about you

CARTER: (*Laughs*) Yes, I am aware of this, but in my opinion the pros for remain outweigh the cons. And the House knows this

POPPY: Well I've pitched a referendum to the big wigs and they all agree next summer would be perfect

CARTER: We can't make any decisions if we're not in the EU

POPPY: The majority of the Cabinet want to put this forward

CARTER: What did George say?

POPPY: He said the people should vote

CARTER: Yes... but do pigs know what shit they should be eating?

POPPY: That's for them to decide

(*Silence*)

CARTER: Fine. Put it through

POPPY: (*Overjoyed*) Thanks babe, really appreciate it yeah

(*She exits. Silence. Glyniss death stares Carter*)

CARTER: (*Obnoxiously*) What?

GLYNISS: (*Beat*) Think you're funny do you? (*Advancing on him*) Funny funny man

CARTER: What are you driving at here?

GLYNISS: You put her in charge of Europe. Showing off again are we David?

CARTER: Is this about the treasury thing? Oh! Poppy... right. Okay. I see

GLYNISS: What?

CARTER: The whole middle-aged thing

GLYNISS: Were you loved as a child? I'm genuinely asking, for that would explain your disgusting insecurity and colossal failure as a human being? Do you remember when I first took you on David, all those years ago? A promising, young junior cabinet officer always wanting my approval

CARTER: Yes, time has been terribly cruel to your face hasn't it?

(*Silence*)

(*Laughs uncomfortably*) What?

GLYNISS: Let's not forget who's really in charge shall we?

CARTER: Yeah, me

GLYNISS: No. I think you need reminding

CARTER: (*Worried*) No no, I don't think I do actually

GLYNISS: (*Defiant*) No I really think you do (*She advances*)

CARTER: (*Trying to escape*) Glyniss what are you doing?

GLYNISS: Someone has got a little too big for their boots

CARTER: (*Pleading*) Seriously, back off!

GLYNISS: Someone needs a good old prod!

(*She grabs Carter, they wrestle. It's violent, aggressive and weird. She is deceptively very strong. She ties his arm round his back, and bends him over the desk*)

Now admit I'm bloody in charge!

CARTER: No (*She wrenches his arm tighter, Carter wails. It is quite painful*)

GLYNISS: Now admit it you over-privileged regency prick

CARTER: Yeah that's it, ride me like a donkey

GLYNISS: Don't you bloody dare

CLOG: (*Entering*) I've bought you a Frappuccino as way of an apology

(*Silence. No one knows what to say*)

CLOG: (*Timidly*) Room for a third?

(*Silence*)

GLYNISS: I'm in charge. Don't you ever forget that (*She exits*)

(*Silence*)

CLOG: Caramel Frappuccino? (*Places it gingerly on the desk*)

(*Silence*)

(*Can't resist*) Don't do it Dave she'll break your heart (*Carter exits*) She's a maneater

(*Patrick comes rushing in, the phones are going mental, it's all kicked off*)

PATRICK: Glyniss! (*Poppy enters*)

POPPY: What is it, what's the matter?

PATRICK: Contraband's blown the lid off, he's announcing the proposition of a coalition with the Scots

POPPY: (*Perplexed*) What is he doing?

PATRICK: Either he fears getting the majority or he's creating allies to gain him more votes

POPPY: Which he'll drop like a sack of shit post results

(*Glyniss enters frantically, on the phone*)

GLYNISS: Patrick!

PATRICK: Did you hear?

GLYNISS: Yes! He's mind fucking us the little fucker

PATRICK: Is he not just panicking?

GLYNISS: No no no it's a trap! He has no intention of any coalition

POPPY: Shall I call the press?

GLYNISS: Yes (*To Patrick*) But what do we say in response?

PATRICK: We can't respond just after Labour, that looks like we're panicking

CLOG: We mustn't panic! We mustn't panic!

POPPY: I don't think we should call the press at all

GLYNISS: But we're behind, Dave won't consider joining anyone

CLOG: I think we should genuinely consider the Green Party as an option. They really are the up and comers, the Luke Skywalker of the political world… the Newcastle United if you will, the young salmon travelling up the stream if I can stretch / my metaphor

GLYNISS: Shut up Nick!

PATRICK: Let's label his insecurity, he has no confidence in gaining a majority and doesn't trust his voters

GLYNISS: Yes, very good. We don't call a press conference, we just say we won't even discuss a coalition scenario till post results, we don't need to

PATRICK: We have full confidence in our voters

GLYNISS: That'll work. Poppy! Just alert a few journos, we don't want to make a big song and dance about this (*She gets on her phone*)

PATRICK: The whole point Poppy is to make out we don't care; we're not bothered by it

POPPY: I'll need you to prep Dave, the press will be outside No. 10 in 20

PATRICK: No, he mustn't come out and announce it, that'll look like we're responding. They need to catch him accidentally on the way out

GLYNISS: And when questioned he gives a very short, detailed, well delivered sentence that doesn't looked manufactured or rehearsed at all. Christ! What if they question him about Morgan's death?

PATRICK: (*He thinks*) Okay... Then let's make it about Morgan... Dave comes out and they bombard him with Contraband, coalitions and decapitated journalists. His response is he will not give even a second thought to coalitions until the fundamentalists are found

GLYNISS: And the Morgans are paid compensation for their loss?

CLOG: No that's pissing on his grave

GLYNISS: No one asked you Tiny Tim

CLOG: I'm sorry for your loss, here's twenty grand a year and the PM will give you a cuddle on the 10 o'clock news (*He exits*)

PATRICK: He's right, it's too try hard. Finding the assailants and killing them comes across as genuine and patriotic. Get the car round to pick him up so it looks like he's going somewhere

GLYNISS: Also he can escape if he fluffs it up

POPPY: Where shall I tell the driver to take him?

GLYNISS: I don't know, it doesn't bloody matter, dump him in a ditch off the M11

PATRICK: Where is he now?

GLYNISS: Don't worry about him, he's having a word with himself… Right! (*Addresses the audience*) Listen in people. The race to the GE is well on its way! There are long, hard, dark days ahead. File your divorces, we're pulling an all-nighter. I want a presentation by 7am tomorrow of all possible, impossible, likely, and ridiculous electoral results scenarios. Even one involving the BNP and the Hitler Youth. We need to prepare for anything this time, no stone unturned! Paddy prep Dave, and I want a rundown of all Conservative policies v Labour, you know the drill… any comparisons, we promise more and better! (*Turns to Patrick*) Christ we've got a lot of work to do… I feel like Mel Gibson's lawyer in Tel Aviv

PATRICK: We can't do this chess game for weeks, we need to stand out with hard policies

GLYNISS: Oh thanks for that, because those game changing election policies are ten a penny aren't they?

PATRICK: Then make Social Welfare our priority, make our agenda clear and concrete, no one can argue with that

(*Clog enters*)

CLOG: I have some valuable information regarding the Rebel Alliance

GLYNISS: Piss off Stuart Little

CLOG: Oh okay, well if you really wanna know Contraband isn't just going to promise more than we can deliver and launch class warfare

GLYNISS: We know that you daft prat

CLOG: Oh fine by me, you know what you're doing. But if you don't want to hear the leak that Ned's not playing by the rules, your funeral

GLYNISS: Of course they are going to leak false information you muppet

CLOG: Oh you know it then! Oh okay, sorry to bother

GLYNISS: The opposition wouldn't leak self-sabotaging info?

PATRICK: Ned's opposition are within his own party

GLYNISS: But they would never leak this to you of all people

PATRICK: Yes but they hate Ned, his cabinet don't have any confidence in him

CLOG: They're already organising a regicide

GLYNISS: Bollocks, he's the "Lost Prince"

CLOG: All I know is he's not as popular as the media make him out to be

PATRICK: There's revolt amongst his troops, he's coming across as a disgruntled child that can't handle the pressure

CLOG: They've got a PR company working day and night; they've gone all King's Speech on him

GLYNISS: Your point being?

CLOG: My point being is that he's a complete electoral nightmare, his cabinet want him to fall flat on his face. His only strategy is to go for Carter no holds barred, picking at any weaknesses

PATRICK: Exposing all the wrongdoing and mistakes the right has created in the last five years

CLOG: (*Sings*) But it's fine it's fine it's fine!

GLYNISS: Put the kettle on would you Nick

(*He exits, Carter storms in*)

CARTER: He's bottled it. He's a flake, a lightweight, a political and social disaster

GLYNISS: Had a word with yourself did we?

CARTER: Yes ma'am… it shan't happen again

GLYNISS: Too right it won't. You know what he's up to?

CARTER: Up to? He's got as much subtly and grace as two gorillas fucking (*Addressing the audience*) I see you Ned Contraband, I see you. You are drowning my friend. You think you're Moses leading the Israelites to the Promised Land, and I'm the Pharaoh? I'm your Jehovah motherfucker!

(*Lights down. Two spotlights up. One on Carter, the other on a strange figure in a brown cloak, pushing a mop. An old man with white hair and a beard… Obi Wan?*)

CORBZ: The truth will out; I can feel it in the Atmos Sphere

CARTER: I'm sorry?

CORBZ: The game's afoot. One will fall, one will rise. But both are marked men

CARTER: Sorry are you with catering?

CORBZ: The dragon shall be slain. The whale beached. The pelican will squawk its last word. The Ewok shall touch itself ever so gently in the darkness one last time

CARTER: Are you on some sort of day pass?

CORBZ: From the ashes arises the Phoenix

(*Blackout*)

(*Lights up. The Red Party's Headquarters, Westminster. Their leader Ned Contraband, stands centre stage. He is of Jewish heritage, wears no shoes, socks or jacket. He just stands there transfixed, staring into the middle distance. Silence. Music plays, Ned starts prancing round the room, dancing very expressively with his strip of red tie, it's wild and strange, has he lost the plot? While this takes place, Sharon Slaughter has entered. She is an intense, stylish woman. She watches Contraband, stunned. Sharon smashes the disc player*)

(*Silence*)

SHARON: What are you doing?

NED: I'm...I'm releasing myself

SHARON: Well you look like a cunt

NED: Sorry, who are you?

SHARON: I'm Merry Poppins mate, I'm your fairy poof Mother and I'm here to make you famous sunshine

NED: (*Concerned*) Where's Will, I want Will?

SHARON: Will isn't here right now, It's just me (*Threateningly*) *you* and *me*

NED: I was warming up

SHARON: Will is no longer solely responsible for coaching you in this election. We've got eight weeks, and so far you've been a complete fucking disaster. You're a no-hoper, the party has written you off

NED: I think you'll find *love* I'm doing just fine, the polls are very tight

SHARON: No one's voting for you son, they're gonna vote for change, not some daft prat who can't tell the difference between his thumb and his dick

NED: How bloody dare you! I'm not listening to this. (*He puts his shoes and socks back on*) I want Will, he's good, he's kind to me and says I'm doing really well

SHARON: Well no... You've got me right now

NED: What is this, I demand to know who sent you?

SHARON: Your cabinet don't feel a hundred percent confident in Will's methods. They fear if they don't act now, it will be too late. That Feng Shui, Lapsang Souchong drinking prancing pony is indisposed and not available to you at this present time. You've got me, Mazel tov!

NED: I have quite sufficient aide, thank you (*Goes to leave*)

SHARON: Or shall I give the Shadow Cabinet a little call Ned?

(*He freezes. Silence*)

NED: You wouldn't dare

SHARON: Shall I get my Blueberry out and call the Dark Lord. Oooooooooo you wouldn't want that now would you? Shall I call Lord Mangleson? Oh he'd love you wouldn't he. (*Ned is petrified*) Tell him to stop writing his memoirs and say I've got a nice juicy prick here that's leading Labour into oblivion?

(*Silence*)

Make the right choice

NED: (*Hysterically*) But how can I trust you?

SHARON: I'm here to stop you fudging up no more. Because right now you're coming across like a pork pie in a Synagogue. No one wants you here. I'm here to fix you Ned, can I call you Ned? I'm here to make a Prime Minister out of you this country deserves. You have presented in front of you the golden opportunity. Enough of all this hippie shit and start being an actual candidate for office with cast iron bollocks and skin as hard as nails, whadya say?

(*Silence*)

NED: I'm fine, thank you

SHARON: Really? Sure about that? That's not what's been whispered round Westminster

NED: What! What do you mean, what are they saying?

SHARON: You're a joke, a fiend and a cretin

NED: How dare you!

SHARON: They wanted to boot you out weeks ago, but your nearest and dearest loyal dogs have sworn by you, but I'm not gonna lie Ned… I don't like you. You're a terrible politician. You're the miscarriage, the afterbirth. Your brother… excellent! Top lad, right choice. You know what I think when I see you…? They got it wrong. You're a waste, a mediocre candidate for a super heavyweight role. I'm not being rude, I'm just being honest. No one likes you. If we were to draw a diagram of the human anatomy and each MP has a function, I would be the heart. If you removed me, you're finished. With me, you'll keep on going till you're meant to stop. You however, are the sphincter, the arse hole. Because the anus decides how much shit stays in, and how much shit goes out. Think you're insignificant, oh no, you're imperative. No one wants to give the sphincter all this power, but unfortunately he's got it. And he can decide right now to store up all the shit he likes and intoxicate and poison the whole body, infecting his entire party. Or… he can decide to let rip, and clear the bowels of all the rot. Do you know why I'm the way I am Ned? It's because I haven't shat in five years. That's a lot of rot isn't it? Release me Ned, release my sphincter and let's shit all over those posh twats together and run this country, whadya say pal?

NED: Yeah, let's do it! Let's fuck this posh twat right up the arse hole!

SHARON: That's the spirit (*They shake hands vigorously*) Right, we haven't got long. You're doing okay, not great but okay. According to my sources, you're two percent ahead of the Tories, and you're the youngest Labour leader ever. You're fresh, exciting, and moderately attractive in a Pingu sort of way, so let's talk image

NED: I know I'm sorry, my wife dresses me, she's a very boring woman

SHARON: Nah, we'll talk about camouflage later, I'm talkin' about projection

NED: Yes vocal projection, Will says I sit at the back of my larynx

SHARON: I'm not talking about that, I'm talking about *you*. How *you* come across. Let's rid ourselves of this New Labour hashtag. The fat sweaty Scotsman raved about you like you were his love child, but you need to understand the *working man*. Just because you watch EastEnders and shop at Iceland doesn't mean you understand normal people

NED: I want to be characterised as a salt of the earth type

SHARON: Exactly! But also you're a bit of a teacher's pet, a golden boy, but more importantly, you're safe, do you wanna know why?

NED: Why?

SHARON: Because you're boring, you're as dull as Tim Henman. You're a square and as predictable as Kerry Katona bending over and flashing her rat for the paparazzi. You're mediocre at everything; your wife has to endure your bland, mediocre love making, twenty seconds of missionary then "Goodnight darling"

NED: Now that's hardly fair, I'm a sexy guy

SHARON: No you're not. But that's good because it means you're a safe bet. During the expenses scandal you were one of the saints that came out of it. Whilst politicians were on yachts, sipping Dom Perignon, fixing their houses, buying a new Jag, or paying rent boys to shit on their face, you were just going about your business

NED: Of course, electoral candidates can't have their underwear up the flagpole

SHARON: You can honestly tell me there is literally no dirt they can get you with? No skeletons whatsoever?

NED: No, nothing

SHARON: (*Pressing*) Are you absolutely sure?

NED: No I'm clean

SHARON: There's nothing in your past that could bite us in the arse further down the line? No illegitimate inbred bastards running around or dead hooker underneath some floorboards somewhere?

(*Silence*)

What, what is it?

NED: (*Ashamed*) Well there was this one incident

SHARON: Tell. Me. Now

NED: Well… well when I was eighteen, I made out with my first cousin Miriam at a Bar Mitzvah

SHARON: Were you drunk?

NED: No

(*Silence*)

I did… I did also do a half marathon with Jimmy Saville when I was 13

(*Silence*)

It was for charity! And I have nothing to complain about, he was nothing but charming

(*Silence*)

SHARON: It's very important you stop being you Ned. Just for now. At this present moment in time just shut your mouth, learn the script, don't ad lib, your life depends on it

NED: But shouldn't the public know who I really am?

SHARON: No! The British Public will never in their right mind vote for an imbecilic buffoon like you. You're a national joke, everyone feels you're just an interim leader till the next posh twat who can't dress comes along. Prove them wrong. Do you really think Churchill wasn't a racist, bigoted, sexist arse behind closed doors? The public adored him because he gave them what they wanted at that moment in time and won them the war. In politics, Never Be You

NED: But Will says "always be true to yourself"

SHARON: Will's a nonce! A hemp wearing special needs sex pest that shouldn't even be here. You need to stop this touchy feely bollocks and be more cut-throat. Go for Carter's jugular

NED: I'm not going to lie to win over the disaffected

SHARON: I never said lie, statistics don't lie. The truth is concrete. Accuse him of being guilty of practicing old policies and breaking his promises

NED: He's sacrificed everything on deficit reduction

SHARON: Yes! Now we're cooking, what else?

NED: He pledged to reduce migrants yet the statistics say almost treble that entered the country last year

SHARON: What are my three magic words Ned... "Immigration, Immigration, Immigration" Everyone in the UK is terrified about losing their jobs, money, housing to the foreigners, the aunty that never leaves after Christmas, the fat pigeon on the street that refuses to budge

NED: Corruption within the party! He hired the former editor of *"Views of the World"*, paying him a hundred and fifty grand a year

SHARON: He's a phone hacker and a weasel. Go on about the hacks, and how sick and twisted it is

NED: I could suggest the Tories need an internal inquiry?

SHARON: Even suggest the PM's been at it too?

NED: Oh no, that's too far

SHARON: Come on Ned smell the blood for Christ's sake

NED: It was never proved

SHARON: Then why did he hire the editor… what could he possibly need him for?

(*Silence. Ned slowly removes a crumpled newspaper clipping from his wallet, he's clearly had it on him for a while*)

NED: David Carter once said "I did lots of things before I came into politics I shouldn't have done, we all did"

SHARON: Well done Sméagol. When a diamond like this just simply lands in your lap, you cash it in for all it's worth

NED: What do you mean?

SHARON: With this you could suggest literally anything

NED: Like what?

SHARON: Be creative. You could even say he sodomised a sheep at a wedding in Kent if you like

NED: No one will believe something that hideous!

SHARON: (*Beat*) Won't they...? They'll believe what we tell them mate. And they'll believe anything

NED: Yes, I like it. I feel naughty and dirty

SHARON: Yeah?

NED: (*Excited*) Yeah!

SHARON: Get in amongst the filth with the others; lob a grenade into the social arena

NED: I could say Carter doesn't pay any tax!

SHARON: That's the spirit, plant seeds of doubt into the voters. We need to pressure him into this TV debate

NED: No that was a terrible idea, I regret what I said

SHARON: Come on Edward, back yourself. You threw down the gauntlet, ask for a shoot-out

NED: I got cocky about the Morgan inquiry, besides he'll destroy me on live TV, you've seen him, he's great on camera. I just sweat profusely and feel like I need a poo

SHARON: Why do you think I'm here? I'll coach you Ned; I'll Yoda you so hard and hit you with some knowledge that even Jeremy Pac-man will be terrified of interviewing you

NED: How?

SHARON: We just pump out to the media all these outrageous accusations, then call him up on it, live… in front of millions. Let him squirm

NED: Yes!

SHARON: So tomorrow we'll leak to the press that he sexually propositioned Ann Widdecombe or something. Now, off the cuff let's briefly fire out coalition possibilities. How do you feel about Nigel Garage and UKRAP?

NED: No, absolutely not

SHARON: Oh he loves you

NED: No! Every red will be turning in their grave if I do the Macarena with him

SHARON: Look, I know he's a twat ranting about the Poles and Romanians, but people do get him

NED: He's a watered down white supremacist for God's sake

SHARON: Well what about the Greens?

NED: Sharon, they're a complete shambles and only Shoreditch hipster wankers vote Green. What about the Scottish Nationals, Salmon likes me, he said that on the television

SHARON: A Labour SNP Government…? That's Nightmare on Elm Street son. They're the marmite of the political world, trust me give a wide berth… Why not the Liberals? They cross over on so many things

NED: No! They've got no integrity, which is the worst thing I can say about anyone

SHARON: Yes, but the Tories will get in simply because there isn't an equal alternative, we need possible coalition options

NED: But do you not feel that's wrong, that we've cheated our way in…? Clog was right, our voting system's completely broken

SHARON: Yes. We know this. It's been broken for years, but it ain't gonna change. Right now, I need you to do what I say, word for word

NED: I will Sharon, I promise

SHARON: Good. But they're gonna go for you boy, you do realise that don't you? I mean look at you, you look ridiculous, where did you get that suit, Mothercare? Now stand up straight and be the leader this country deserves. (*He does so*) Be that man Ned, be the guy representing all those people that kept on going. The nurses, the teachers on minimum pay, the small business going bust, the corner shop owner, the factory workers. Labour just keeps on going. Now say "I belong here"

NED: I belong here

SHARON: Like you mean it you poof

NED: I belong here

SHARON: No you don't!

NED: I belong here!

SHARON: You're a slug!

NED: (*With feeling*) I belong here!

SHARON: You were an accident

NED: (*Upset*) I belong here!

SHARON: Your brother should be here not you!

NED: (*Inner Rage*) NO...! I belong here! I belong here! I BELONG HERE!

SHARON: Yes! That's it! Now I see a Leader, now I care! Now I see the ruthless politician who stabbed his brother in the back

(*Will enters unnoticed. He is barefoot, wears Thai fisherman trousers, a hemp jumper and carries with him a drum. He is a tender and very spiritual man. He adores and sees great potential in Ned*)

SHARON: And what are you going to do to Carter?

NED: Ruin him

SHARON: How?

NED: Trample him, rip his throat out, scandalise him!

SHARON: Yes!

NED: I'm going to kill that posh wanker!

WILL: Ned?

NED: (*Horrified*) Will

WILL: What's going on Ned?

NED: (*Very unsure*) I'm… I'm going to kill the Prime Minister

WILL: But what about *the love* Ned… all that work we did on *the love*

SHARON: God 'ere we go

NED: Yes, the love… I'm, I'm scared Will. I'm confused… I don't know who I am anymore (*He starts to cry*)

WILL: Shhhhhhhh, No no no, what is this? What have you done to him? Enough of this silliness (*He embraces him*) so much pain Ned. So much rage

SHARON: Jesus fuck

NED: (*Blubbing*) She told me to do it

WILL: You're getting a lot of information aren't you?

NED: Overwhelmingly so

WILL: We all think you're doing really well, so brave

NED: Really?

WILL: I don't use the word "Hero" a lot Ned, but you young man are right up there. I'm so incredibly proud of you, aren't we Sharon? So incredibly proud

SHARON: I've never been so professionally embarrassed to represent such a train wreck of a leader

NED: She's right, I'm a complete disaster. When Carter speaks he means it, he's got authority, I'm useless

WILL: No you're not useless, you're developing

SHARON: Developing into a prize time twat

WILL: Well that's not very nice is it?

NED: Here lies Ned Contraband, backstabber, political flop and prize time twat (*Cries again*)

WILL: Hey! What? No, shhhhhh (*Embraces him*) don't listen to her, listen to me. Ned, look at me (*Holds his head, it's odd*) I love you, yeah? I believe in you, now do you believe in yourself?

NED: Yes

WILL: (*Smiling*) There we go, there you are, there's my leader

NED: A loving leader

WILL: Very good, let's just warm you up shall we and get some vocal release, how you feeling?

NED: Nervous Will, and sad, so very sad

WILL: Of course, why wouldn't you be (*Will starts working on him, massaging his body*) There we go, Oh! Who's that? That's new (*He massages out the knot*) let's get rid of him shall we (*He then brushes*

off the negative energy and stands back from him) There we go, that's better. Think long spine, release that jaw (*He does so*) very good

SHARON: (*To the audience*) Have I joined the Scientologists?

WILL: Ignore the haters and the negativities

SHARON: Is this one of Kevin Spacey's after parties?

NED: I feel stupid Will

WILL: Don't listen to her now, she's not important, just focus on me, me and the work

NED: "The work in the room"

WILL: Everything else is irrelevant. Say the mantra, say it

NED: I am the captain of my own ship and every day in every way I'm getting stronger, harder and sexier

WILL: Yes, yes you are. Now close your eyes and listen to my coaching (*He picks up his drum and starts beating*) listen to my voice... And breathe... now roll down into downward facing dog, excellent, great form Ned, just going to absorb some of your energy (*He hugs him from behind. It's very strange*) such positive energy (*He detaches*)

SHARON: (*On her phone*) This is what yoga classes in Broadmoor are like

WILL: Now from dog roll up into marmoset, then plant yourself, very good, now into starfish and show me your glorious tentacles... now shake it off! (*He does so aggressively, Will beats his drum louder and faster*) Now we're metamorphosing quickly through the exploration of emotions through the void of glorious Technicolor... Listen to the beat and let it change and inform you organically (*He beats louder and faster. Ned starts jerking suddenly and violently, an interpretive dance. It's exotic and unnerving*) Now we're entering the red zone... not anger but passion (*Ned completely loses the plot, is he having a breakdown?*) Now fly pelican fly...! Yes that's it! You're a monkey, a dirty little ape (*Ned suddenly turns into a chimp*) go monkey go! (*Ned destroys the room as a chimp, flipping chairs over, into the audience. He goes for Sharon*) No! Bad monkey bad! (*Will slaps his hand. Chimp Ned flips out*) and relax (*Will beats his drum once, Ned falls to the floor shaking*) Now rise (*He does so*) now open your eyes. How do you feel? (*Ned just stands there, docile*) Very good Ned. Now just find a bit of text from your speech, any bit, doesn't matter, and intone it

(*Silence*)

NED: VOICE! (*Sings*) To the left to the left, Everything that you own in a box to the left

WILL: Excellent projection, now in your own time start your speech

(*Silence*)

NED: (*With great conviction*) Is this a dagger which I see before me, the handle toward my hand? Come, let me clutch thee. I have thee not, and yet I / see thee still

WILL: That was really good Ned, very positive. When I said speech, I was referring to your political speech. Do you remember that speech Ned? Do you know who you are Ned?

NED: ....

SHARON: Christ he's cracked it, he's lost the plot. This is a complete shambles

WILL: No this is good, it's progress

SHARON: Look what you've done, you've turned him into a potato, he's not fit to take a dump by himself let alone run the country

WILL: He's developing

SHARON: He's losing the election you fucking hippie

(*Silence*)

WILL: Mate, I'm not going to lie. Your energy is quite negative, aggressive and incredibly destructive to my kinesphere. I'm going to have to ask you to step out of the temple

SHARON: The what?

WILL: The fortress of love... Ned came up with it

SHARON: Let me make one thing perfectly crystal clear happy hands. If you fudge this political campaign up and tarnish my party, I will make it my life's ambition to make sure you are put on every sex case register from Inverness to Penzance, you will be blacklisted for all eternity, understood Polanski?

WILL: My process takes time

SHARON: If we don't see a substantial improvement in the next three days, I'm going to get Brutus, Cassius and all the other senators to don their robes, sharpen their blades, and pull Ned Contraband from this election... Have I made myself transparently clear you tree-groping twat?

WILL: I command you leave the sanctum

SHARON: Not on my watch bummer boy

(*They stare each other down. Will breaks off*)

WILL: Ned?

NED: (*Coming out of his trance, in a hypnotic state*) Yes William?

WILL: How are you feeling?

NED: (*As if he's heavily drugged*) Oh I don't feel anything anymore. I'm just a sponge... a floppy floppy sponge

WILL: Now that's not true is it now Ned. You're a hero. (*Beat*) There's a hero, if you look inside your heart, you don't have to be afraid of what you are. There's answer, if you reach into your soul, and the sorrow that you know will melt away...

NED: (*Sings*) and then a hero comes along, with the strength to carry on

WILL: Yes that's it!

NED: (*Growing confidence*) and you cast your fears aside, and you know you must survive

WILL: Back yourself now!

NED: (*With great passion*) so when you feel like hope is gone, look inside you and be strong

SHARON: I can't fucking believe this (*She exits*)

NED: And you'll finally see the truth, that a hero lies in you

(*Silence*)

WILL: Do the speech

(*Beat*)

NED: People of Britain. There is something very wrong with this country. That's one thing we can all agree on despite race, class or creed. We have proven to the world we are an incredible nation with fantastic people. Brave, courageous, charismatic, hardworking folk who are open and flexible to change, what an absolute tragedy our government does not reflect this mighty Isle. My sole aim is to serve these people. Yes I will make mistakes, yes I will frustrate people, yes I will be caught eating bacon sandwiches in an unflattering and disgruntled manner, but I will not fail you. If elected, it will be my job, with every fibre of my being to absolutely deliver on any promise I make, pick a Cabinet who actually want me there, to set greater goals than simply reducing the deficit through overtaxing and cuts, to make people proud to live in this wonderful country that has such boundless potential. David Carter will give you no alternative but to vote for him. Will promise unrealistic policies he simply won't deliver. He will ridicule me on the basest level in a cheap attempt to swing uncertain voters simply because I don't fit the bill as Party Leader. Well groomed, entitled, egotistical, over privileged, arrogant, a compulsive liar and above all, a coward. Surely now it is time to break that mould? I will never make a promise I am not certain I can guarantee, what's the point, who benefits from that? And I swear, unlike my predecessors, if I do not deliver or achieve my policies, I will resign. Simply because a leader must be selfless at all times, put aside their ego, for the people they serve deserve only the very best. I ask you not to vote for the Tories simply because they're already in office, but take the risk of choosing the only alternative. Ask not "what about what I need?" Ask yourself "what do we all need?" For a society is a collective. Britain, I am here to serve you.

(*Silence*)

WILL: (*Overwhelmed*) I can't, I mean… just wow Ned! I love you. How did that feel?

NED: It felt right… honest

WILL: Absolutely. This is who you are, this is how you're gonna lead. No lies, no bullshit. Unbiased, truthful honesty

NED: Yeah (*Sharon enters, overjoyed*)

SHARON: Right golden boy we're going over the top. I have just been leaked the motherlode of all political atomic bombs. Ned, tonight young man is your lucky night

WILL: Sorry Sharon we're just in/ the middle of

SHARON: When I drop this Edward, Carter will resign before the week is out, which means old sport, Clog is in charge, and you'll absolutely dismantle him in the ballots

NED: What, what is it?

SHARON: Oh the horror, the beautiful beautiful horror

NED: What?

SHARON: The depravity of the PM's past coming back to devour his arse

NED: Sorry?

SHARON: Two words. Lord Ainsworth

NED: What about Lord Ainsworth?

SHARON: His new biography of our mate Dave and his posh twat club

WILL: Don't get poisoned Ned!

NED: Is he spilling the beans about Oxford?

WILL: The work is at its most crucial point/ and you bring

SHARON: Now listen here sex pest, I've indulged your cultish methods for far too long, this is an election campaign not a gap year in Bali

WILL: That's not very nice

SHARON: From now on I'm head coach of Ned, you understand Tinkerbell? We need to take advantage of this situation for all it's worth and I don't need you mind-fucking him

NED: Lord Ainsworth you beautiful bastard!

SHARON: Press conference at one, you're gonna force his resignation

WILL: What about the love Ned?

SHARON: Shut up you

NED: We'll work on it later I promise

SHARON: This is our chance Ned, the Reds are coming back to No. 10! Let's milk this for every mother and her son (*Sharon exits, shouting down the phone, Will protests after her. Ned is left alone*)

NED: Unbiased, truthful honesty… what's the point? (*Suddenly it goes dark, a figure in a brown cloak appears. He is brushing the floor with a broom, he pulls down his hood, it's the wise janitor*)

CORBZ: There is always a point Edward, honesty and truth are concrete, lies and games are not

NED: I just don't know who I am anymore Jez… I want to be me, but maybe me isn't good enough to run this country

CORBZ: Seek to help, not to please. Always be true to yourself

NED: But does the truth win an election campaign?

CORBZ: Trust yourself, do not fear Carter

NED: But will I win?

CORBZ: One will fall and one will rise

NED: What the fuck are you on about? No one in this place makes any bloody sense, and why are you sweeping the floor?

CORBZ: I'm cleaning up your mess… metaphorically (*Ned turns his back to him*)

NED: (*Jez drifts away*) But everyone wants me to lose, no one will give me a chance. Do I listen to Will and be honest, or be a bitch like Sharon and win

(*He turns around*) I'm just so confused... Jez? (*Blackout*)

(*No. 10, the very same evening. Nick Clog is sitting crossed legged on the floor building an Airfix model on some newspaper. He has several documents round him, empty take away boxes and a glass of milk. He doesn't care anymore. Patrick enters*)

PATRICK: Nick I need your signature for, oh...! Sorry... are you busy?

CLOG: Patrick hi!

PATRICK: I can come back/ later

CLOG: No come on in old chap, just finishing off the wings on the Luftwaffe

PATRICK: Why aren't you working in your office?

CLOG: Oh I haven't got one. Dave prefers me to work on the floor like a dog... he calls me his little cocker spaniel WOOF! WOOF! (*He laughs uncomfortably*)

(*Silence*)

PATRICK: How's preparation going for the Lib Dem's campaign Nick?

CLOG: I don't really know, they tend to keep me out of the loop these days on pretty much everything

(*Silence*)

PATRICK: You know you're the only reason I went into politics

CLOG: Oh! You're very kind

PATRICK: I mean it. You guys were... are... great. The closest party that represents the majority. Selfless, honest and uncorrupted. Lobbying reformation on proportional representation was genius

CLOG: Ah yes, the votes actually counting

PATRICK: A party advocating political revolution that this country so desperately needs (*Beat*) What happened to you Nick?

CLOG: I'm sorry?

PATRICK: When did you stop caring?

(*Nick lets out a big long sigh*)

CLOG: I didn't. David did. I mean you've seen him, in the end he just flattered me with the title. At first he listened to my ideas and then just stopped acknowledging my existence altogether. I was played Pat

PATRICK: But you were so popular, what happened to "Clogmania"?

CLOG: I dug my own grave. They said I was the next Churchill, then why didn't they vote for me? I tell you, secret Tories are the killer... God my campaign was good! I could have changed literally everything but the voting system royally screwed me. How can that be, that's not a democracy?

PATRICK: (*Passionately*) But that's why you wanted to reform Nick, you can still get votes, win them back for God's sake! Distance yourself from the Tories, cut off the cancer and get out there. The Liberal Democrats are about the little guys

CLOG: No... I can't even if I wanted to. I lost all respect as soon as I entered this cesspit. He turned me into a traitor and imposter, Dave and his fucking cabinet. A pitiful coward making a flimsy deal with the Devil. God why wasn't I patient, I should have waited

PATRICK: You panicked and sold out

CLOG: We all did. Bloody Carter... he said there were overlaps, policy crossovers, similarities, there weren't. There was no flexibility, no compassion! We're two completely different species. It was the Nazi-Soviet pact all over again. It was him that ultimately needed us. I should've gone with Gordan, the fat sweaty Scotsman and I were more alike

PATRICK: But the promises, were they accurate? Eight billion against cuts? Lowering tuition fees? Why did you compromise everything?

CLOG: That was the deal. Besides, I lied about promises we weren't absolutely sure we could deliver. It's always easy to be against something, pointing out the fault. But once you're in the castle you realise there really is no money, cuts are a necessity. Why didn't I back myself...? Lack of confidence I suppose

PATRICK: You regret the coalition?

CLOG: It happened in Seventy Four, Maggie said "No, It's not worth it, be patient" ...Why wasn't I patient? I tell you what: George Oblong twisted Dave round his little finger, he masterminded the whole thing. Don't ever be seduced Patrick by Carter and his cronies. It's the ones lurking in the shadows behind closed doors that are really running this country. There's no such thing as democracy. The system was broken and I failed to fix it

PATRICK: There's still time Nick, your party is still strong/go on the televised

(*Glyniss comes storming in; she is in a fury, followed by Poppy and Carter. The campaign is not going well*)

GLYNISS: Paddy! Why did you tweet that twat on twatter, what the hell is wrong with you?

PATRICK: For what sorry?

GLYNISS: Don't give me that, the one about us not cancelling the People's Medical Service?

PATRICK: What's wrong, because I spoke the truth? That's what we promised!

GLYNISS: You have ninety thousand followers for Christ sake, it's in the Standard

CARTER: Is that true JD Sports?

CLOG: Yes, as far as it goes the public think we're not cutting it

GLYNISS: Jesus Christ! Where do you come off you little shit, what gives you the right?

CLOG: She's right Pat that was reckless. We can't get votes that way then U-turn in six months

GLYNISS: You really are a tit!

CARTER: Whoah, whoah... Let's take it easy Tinky Winky, Dipsy, Laa Laa and Po. Dissension in the ranks of my little Teletubbies

POPPY: What were you thinking? This will bite us so hard in the arse

CARTER: Yes pop star yes!

PATRICK: I was only highlighting what you promised in twenty ten

GLYNISS: By making it public we have to run with it now

CARTER: What have you done Punjabi MC?

POPPY: To go back on it now would be disastrous

CARTER: Well what's the problem, what's the solution? Let's sort it out munchkins

CLOG: Hang on; before we go on... I'm with Paddy on this. The Coalition was adamant that it would never privatise the People's Medical Service

GLYNISS: Oh do shut up, we all know privatisation has been taking place for months

PATRICK: (*Distraught*) Then why did you promise it in the first place when you knew?

CLOG: What are you saying… we simply can't afford it?

POPPY: There's already a one billion deficit, it's not sustainable

CARTER: Yes! Research, well done

PATRICK: I'm sorry that's bollocks, spending on private providers' accounts for six per cent of the total budget

CLOG: Private companies eradicate the key foundations on which the People's Medical Service was established

POPPY: It would only be used for the greater good of the patient, and private companies would not benefit

CLOG: But there's less honesty and transparency

CARTER: Yes Frodo, hit them with some knowledge

CLOG: No one is to be accountable for when private involvement increases

PATRICK: Commercial confidentiality makes it impossible to find blame when all goes to shit

CLOG: Different organisations offering different services means varying standards across Britain

PATRICK: I.e. Newport and Glasgow being the dumps they are will receive the bottom of the barrel healthcare. I'm sorry; I can't help feeling deep inside of me/ many are going to lose out

CARTER: (*Sings*) Ooga chagga, ooga chagga, ooga ooga ooga chagga, I can't stop this feeling/ deep inside of me

GLYNISS: You little boys aren't getting it are you... There isn't any money! The population is increasing and people simply won't die sooner

POPPY: Public spending on healthcare is just going to increase and strain the budget

PATRICK: Private companies are dominated by shareholders. It will be profits before patients. They will overcharge, cut corners on safety picking the most profitable treatments

CLOG: Over seventy five percent of people with mental health issues are not getting treated

PATRICK: Suicide is the biggest killer in the UK for men under fifty. Mental health, it's happening! It's underfunded! And it's a killer

POPPY: But patients will be given more choice so they will pick quality over price

CLOG: Oh I see... you hold a few shares in these companies then?

GLYNISS: Shut up you little pigmy, how do they not win?

POPPY: Whether we get in or not it will still have to be privatised

PATRICK: Then why did you lie you fucking Toffs!

CARTER: Okay, let's wrap this little WI meeting up shall we. Very good guys, very good. At the end of the day boys and girls, Jeremy Cunt has already made his decision. Realistically this can't be solved in parliament. It will take years even if we do deny it on the national TV debates

GLYNISS: You're not going on the debates

CARTER: Er… I'll do what I want sweetheart

POPPY: You have more to lose by taking part

PATRICK: Plus in previous debates you've come across as arrogant and entitled

CLOG: Contraband will remind people of all your broken promises and mistakes in office

CARTER: Isn't that cowardly for me not to accept his challenge? "Dave the debate dodger"

PATRICK: No. He reeks of desperation

POPPY: It will just turn into a pissing contest, you'll mock him, he'll retaliate, no one wins, and everyone doubts voting

PATRICK: And why these two prats are the only option

CARTER: Yeah alright Carphone Warehouse, calm down

GLYNISS: We're not going to talk about the TV debates Dave. We haven't got a stance to take Dave. We haven't event got a consensus on the People's Medical Service/ Dave

CARTER: You and the PMS, I've had it up to here with you and your PMS

GLYNISS: We haven't even discussed possible coalitions. (*David scoffs*) We have to! Every polling station is convinced it will be hung

POPPY: We don't have to go public

CLOG: We'll do private meetings, no one will know

POPPY: Just some possibilities, that's all we need...just in case?

CARTER: Just in case what, we fail?

CLOG: Let's just have coffee and sandwiches on standby

PATRICK: You see... this is exactly what happened before and look at the mess we're in now. Did you or Nick ever think this is where you'd be?

(*Silence*)

CARTER: What are our options?

CLOG: The Greens

CARTER: No

CLOG: They really are very niche

POPPY: It could just be a way to make up the seats

PATRICK: That can't be our sole reason for forming a coalition with them, that's criminal and deceptive to the public

GLYNISS: They're a bunch of sandal wearing tree huggers if you ask me

PATRICK: So they are off the table?

CLOG: Have you considered the Scottish Nationals?

POPPY: Out of the question

PATRICK: They're just a heightened version of Labour and the Tories trying to be different shades of shite, they hate England

CARTER: And they've all got knives, and they're all sniffing glue! Do you remember the last fat sweaty Scotsman ran this country? Oh yeah because that was sensational wasn't it? Literally, what have they got to offer…? Diabetes and deep fried mars bars?

POPPY: Most of their leaders are very young and inexperienced

GLYNISS: They're still in nappies

CLOG: Obnoxious Glaswegian toddlers

CARTER: A deal with the Caledonian massive is strictly off the table

GLYNISS: No we stick with the plan. Exploit voter's patriotic fear of being ruled by the Scots

POPPY: And moral blackmail. If you vote Labour, you're voting the Scots in with them

PATRICK: Right, then that only leaves UKRAP

GLYNISS: Jesus fuck no!

POPPY: Is that what we've come to?

CARTER: They're a PG version of the Nazi party. If the BNP and Wetherspoons had a love child, it would be Nigel Garage

GLYNISS: Fruitcakes, loonies and closet racists

CARTER: Oh I like that line, think I might use it

POPPY: We can't negotiate with Garage

CARTER: It's like communicating to an autistic furby

POPPY: There's also a social stigma, everyone will judge you

PATRICK: What, more than voting for the Tories?

GLYNISS: Their policies are put up borders, control the immigrants and cut foreign aid spending

POPPY: Those are seductive policies to fearful natives

CLOG: It's social suicide

POPPY: The only brutal truth is they say what everyone is thinking

PATRICK: Do they actually though?

POPPY: Whether you like it or not, whatever comes out of Garage's mouth at some point the "everyday man" has said it

GLYNISS: No, we're not going to even entertain this. We toxify his name in the media and make him dangerous to the public

PATRICK: So that's it is it? No allies, no coalitions? Hopefully we get the majority?

CLOG: What do you expect Pat? In this room is concrete evidence that coalitions don't work. Dave and I went against all our political beliefs to form a last minute, slap dash facade of a party. The last five years have been like some hellish pantomime

(*Silence*)

GLYNISS: Moving onto pre-election night and your last televised appearance. This is gold dust for you. Answer all doubts, stamp out any lies and make Contraband look ridiculous

POPPY: With that said, they'll question the economy and how far you're going with public sector cuts?

CARTER: Until we reduce the deficit

PATRICK: People just want it over with. It's been going on for years, when is it going to end?

GLYNISS: We can't possibly predict. We lose money all the time, but deflect questions on cuts and keep hammering home the long term economic plan

PATRICK: And what about the benefits crisis?

POPPY: Now that's getting out of hand

CLOG: People are claiming benefits for drug addiction and obesity

CARTER: We can't keep funding the junkies and the fatties

PATRICK: Right, then we need to completely refigure the entire benefits plan with stricter monitoring

POPPY: People can only claim if they have genuine cases or disabilities

GLYNISS: It's not that simple

CLOG: And we have to reflect that in house. MPs are moaning to get by on eighty K a year when people are genuinely struggling to survive on eight quid an hour

POPPY: What about Greece? Is Europe going to bail them out?

GLYNISS: No

POPPY: Are we?

CARTER: No

PATRICK: Fantastic! Anything else to add to that mein Fuhrer?

CARTER: Hummus! Aphrodite! Taramasalata! Moral of the story is… don't spend what you ain't got

PATRICK: Brilliant

GLYNISS: Now we have to address the dirtiest word on the street right now… immigration

CLOG: God 'ere we go

POPPY: The population has doubled

GLYNISS: We may have to be ruthless on this front

CLOG: Blaming immigrants for the problems within this country is inaccurate and immoral

CARTER: Let's not talk about it

PATRICK: We have to

GLYNISS: Let's just wait and see what Contraband has to say, we haven't got a clear picture yet

PATRICK: We haven't got a clear picture on anything

CLOG: He's right, we can't sidestep these questions with Pac-man, he'll destroy us!

PATRICK: What are we doing about the refugee crisis? Dead bodies are on our very shores as we speak

POPPY: The media can only hide these images for so long

CARTER: How bad actually is it?

GLYNISS: Well ISIS won't stop, we've got to bomb Syria

PATRICK: That can't be the only fucking solution

GLYNISS: Look Sonny Jim…! We need to bomb Syria to stop the Syrians fleeing the bombs and coming here costing Europe hundreds of thousands in unwanted exports pitching up their fucking tents. But we can't however, because the bloody Russians have got there first and the Yanks have been doing it for ages. This subject won't be touched by anyone so don't get into a flap, no one wants to talk about it

CLOG: Are we safe on reprimanding countries with nuclear weaponry?

GLYNISS: Just about, but post-election we need to guilt trip everyone

PATRICK: Right! So condemn our enemies for threatening nuclear arms, yet ignore our allies that have them?

GLYNISS: Do you not realise that the Earth is on the brink of another world war? We must not rock the boat. Yes the Russians, Iranians, North Koreans, Americans and co are behaving abhorrently but we can't get on the wrong side of them

(*Silence*)

POPPY: Environment?

PATRICK: I'll take this one then shall I? Carry on as you are, consume what you like, create another continent of garbage in the Atlantic, ignore the sad fish, keep eating meat, and charge a little bit extra for plastic bags to make us feel better. We are Britain, vote Conservative

(*Silence*)

POPPY: We haven't discussed Labour strategy

GLYNISS: How are we looking?

POPPY: As of last week we're at a dead heat

PATRICK: But statistics means nothing, it's votes that count. You need to get out there and tour the country

GLYNISS: Get in the trench with the plebs and win over the disaffected?

PATRICK: Well that's what Contraband is doing, look at his slogan "Vote Labour to tax the rich and save the PMS" He's becoming a working class hero

CLOG: What?

GLYNISS: There isn't a single working class member in the Labour party

CLOG: He doesn't know a bloody thing about the working man

PATRICK: Unlike you of course

POPPY: The point being whatever he is doing is working, they're winning

GLYNISS: But is this fact though?

PATRICK: The figures don't lie

CARTER: They're wrong. We're not behind, we're six percent ahead

GLYNISS: (*Shocked*) I'm sorry?

(*Beat*)

CARTER: We're six percent ahead and increasing weekly

(*Silence*)

GLYNISS: Sorry, what…? How, how do you know this?

CARTER: Confidential sources

PATRICK: But that's impossible to know if they're ahead?

CARTER: We've got secret access to the Labour shadow cabinet

PATRICK: But, but that sort of information is inaccessible

CARTER: That's because we've been hacking them for weeks

GLYNISS: For God's sake David!

CLOG: We're all complicit now

GLYNISS: Poppy bury it!

POPPY: On it (*She exits*)

PATRICK: What the hell is wrong with you, have you no morals, no shame?

GLYNISS: I don't believe it… I don't fucking believe it

CLOG: If this gets out it puts the whole of parliament in jeopardy (*He exits*)

PATRICK: Corruption on the highest level

CARTER: No one will find out

PATRICK: I'm not listening to this; this is not why I'm here

GLYNISS: You have put the entire party at risk

CARTER: Oh shut up you fucking hypocrites. The fact is hacking happens. That is the privilege we get for being in this special club. We have access to highly private, sensitive, damaging information that can be used as a weapon to eradicate opposition, and scandalise those we don't want in office

PATRICK: But it's illegal David!

CARTER: People hack… all the time. It is what we do. Yes it is illegal, yes it is highly immoral, but it is incredibly sophisticated and we need it to survive. And why do we do it…? Because we can. And we will do anything to get what we want

GLYNISS: Yes but I never want this

PATRICK: This is unspeakable!

CARTER: What? Everyone including you Ghandi at some point in their career has done unspeakable things to get in this room. Leave me and Contraband on an island together and it would be X-rated Lord of the Flies. We would decapitate one another just to get in for another term. And so would both of you

GLYNISS: I wouldn't decapitate myself to get you in

CARTER: Fuck off with that shit! Gilly the only reason you're here is because you destroyed all the female opposition. (*Clog and Poppy enter together reading a large book "Call Me Dave"*)

POPPY: Ummm Dave?

PATRICK: We have to play by the rules

CARTER: Being a boy scout simply doesn't cut it. A first black president choir boy that promised significant change couldn't get anything past the senate.

GLYNISS: Britain is the most advanced civilisation in the World/ and you're

CARTER: We are animals! And we will do horrific things to one another to get what we want. Do not be fooled by the plummy accents, Oxbridge degrees and the Armani suits. We're scavengers waiting to devour one another's flesh. Welcome to politics. I hack, you hack, we all hack... get over it

GLYNISS: (*Gently*) But if this gets out

CARTER: It won't

GLYNISS: I'm not cleaning up your filth

POPPY: (*Terrified*) Dave?

CARTER: What?!

POPPY: Have you seen this?

CARTER: Seen what?

CLOG: (*Overjoyed*) Oh dear David, oh very dear

POPPY: Lord Ainsworth. He's written a biography of you (*She slowly hands him the book, she steps back*)

CARTER: "Call me Dave" Sexy, I like it

POPPY: No David. Page 319

(*He reads. Silence. He stares at the floor. The book drops out of his hands*)

GLYNISS: What is it?

CARTER: (*Frozen*) Oxford (*Beat*) Oxford (*Patrick's phone rings*)

GLYNISS: David what is it? (*Everyone else's phones ring. The world knows*) Oxford, what Oxford? (*Her phone rings. She reads the message. The worst news she could possibly receive*) Oxford!

(*Blackout*)

Act II

(*Ten minutes later. Clog is sitting in Carter's chair, Poppy and Patrick are frantically executing damage control. Carter stands with his face in his hands distraught. Glyniss addresses the audience*)

GLYNISS: Right! All personnel in No. 10 listen very carefully. Former Deputy Chair Lord Ainsworth has made the most ridiculous and heinous accusations against our PM. I will confirm now it is complete and utter bollocks. However, due to his influence people will believe what they read. We are officially at defcon four. Switch off all electrical devices, unhook the main phones immediately, do not answer or send a single email. Anyone caught using any social media will be dismissed with immediate effect. No one is to leave the building for the next forty eight hours, we're on lockdown. We're calling Domino's

CLOG: Yes pizza! Get in!

CARTER: (*Furious*) Get out of my chair

GLYNISS: (*Rapidly*) Poppy fight off the press outside (*She juggles the phones*) Pat tackle the parasites, put a strict embargo of any references to pigs, sows, hogs, boars or fucking swine flu. If they mention anything, heads will roll

PATRICK: I'll get it off social media as well (*Patrick ferociously texts on his phone*)

GLYNISS: I literally have no idea what to say to you, I'm... I'm speechless... You know what actually... Why should I be surprised by you shoving your cock in a pig's mouth? I mean honestly David

CLOG: I really think we should take what Lord Ainsworth says with a pinch of salt, sage and apple sauce (*He chuckles*)

CARTER: Nick! I will literally kill you

GLYNISS: If we don't handle this correctly we could be ruined

CARTER: I am aware of that you silly woman

GLYNISS: Just tell me what you want me to do and I'll sort it

CARTER: I don't know what to do?

GLYNISS: Sorry?

CARTER: What do I do Gilly?

GLYNISS: What's your official statement?

CARTER: I haven't got one

GLYNISS: David... Did you do it? I need to know

CARTER: Did I do what?

GLYNISS: Receive fellatio from a farm animal?

CARTER: Of course I didn't get sucked off by a pig you daft hatchet-faced bint! Oh yes everyone goes ballistic over me shoving my cock in a hog roast when I was nineteen, yet everyone forgets when Ainsworth tossed off a horse in Normandy...! Jesus Christ! Right what are our options? Because I tell you what, if I'm going down I'm taking you all with me. Brainstorm, go!

PATRICK: You fully owning up to what happened and apologising

POPPY: While blaming it on stupidity and peer pressure at an Oxford initiation

PATRICK: Or we could shrug it off? Laugh along with it? Put our hands in the air and surrender to the media onslaught

GLYNISS: No that's stupid

PATRICK: No seriously, we could use it to our advantage, it humanises Dave. So far everyone thinks he's some posh entitled wanker with offshore investments, yet once upon a time (like all of us) he was a silly kid, God knows we've all made mistakes

POPPY: Won't Contraband use it as ammunition?

PATRICK: God no... That's just petulant and desperate

GLYNISS: No I don't like it, it comes across like we've been cornered and it's our only option. Not good enough, what else?

POPPY: Or we completely fly off the handle, absolutely tear the media and public apart, threaten heavy lawsuits and strike a chord of fear in voters and the opposition, we are not to be messed with

CARTER: No, too Nazi party

PATRICK: Well the only option I can see left is you have no choice but to resign. Recovery from this is pretty difficult running up to the election

POPPY: You'll be the laughing stock of Westminster; Nick will be interim PM

CLOG: Oh I like that

CARTER: Nope, not happening

PATRICK: There aren't any other options

CARTER: I don't care what happens, I don't care who dies in the process, sort it out!

(*They all exit. Carter picks up the biography and tears it apart. Suddenly it goes dark. The mysterious hooded figure appears… Obi Wan?*)

CORBZ: The game's afoot… the truth will out

CARTER: What?

CORBZ: The shadows of your past returning to haunt you I see? The orang-utan has slapped the hippo. The penguin and the narwhal have fallen out

CARTER: Wait? What?

CORBZ: One will fall… one will rise (*He disappears*)

(*Carter takes out another phone and makes a call*)

CARTER: Hi George, it's me. It's fucked mate, everything's fucked and I need you... I'm scared George... leave Berlin and come home tonight (*Carter hangs up, Poppy enters*) Poppy! How's things?

POPPY: Ummm... not bad thanks, just trying to save our careers

CARTER: (*Sensing the opportunity*) I find in these times of fear and uncertainty, one can find comfort within their colleagues

POPPY: I don't follow?

CARTER: (*Takes a few steps closer*) I feel we've become friends, close friends. You like me don't you? I'm not just your boss... but at the end of the day, I'm just a man and you're just a woman

POPPY: What are you driving at here?

CARTER: All I'm saying is that we're two little mice lost in a maze... let's find the cheese?

(*Silence*)

POPPY: Are you sexually propositioning me?

CARTER: (Flabbergasted) Sexually proposition

POPPY: Oh let's not shall we? You've wanted me from day one. Sure I'd shag you to get ahead but I don't like you David. I'm not having your porky prick in my vagina

CARTER: Oh don't pretend you don't want it

POPPY: You're going down for this (*She exits swiftly*)

(*Carter is left by himself. He is lost, terrified, close to tears. Glyniss enters*)

GLYNISS: Right I think I have a...

(*Carter grabs Glyniss and gives a long, deep, passionate kiss, Gone With The Wind style, he breaks off*)

CARTER: I know I'm a prick and I take you for granted and don't deserve you but you mean absolutely everything to me

GLYNISS: (*Shocked*) David...

CARTER: You're a falling star, You're a getaway car,
You're the line in the sand when I go too far.
You're the swimming pool on an August day,
And you're the perfect thing to say

(*Beat*)

GLYNISS: Are you quoting Michael Buble... are you attempting to save your political career with Michael Buble?

CARTER: I'm sorry/ I'm just scared

GLYNISS: (*She slaps him hard and grabs him ferociously*) Now you listen here you complete and utter prat. Don't you dare fuck with me David. There is something very wrong with this country and it doesn't take an old Etonian to recognise that. Yes you scrub up very nicely and fit the bill but you are not a politician. You haven't got a clue what this country needs and you are a heartbeat away from coming out of this smelling of roses or pig excrement. Your legacy, our work will be for nothing because of you! My God David you really are an arse. You have the honour to run this country and you behave like this. Now they know who you truly are. You need to wise up my privileged friend because right now you are drowning. Now get out of my sight while I clean up your mess. (*She lets go of him. He just stares at her blubbing*) What?! What's wrong?

CARTER: I've got… I've got an erection

GLYNISS: God's sake

CARTER: I'm sorry I can't help it… I love it when you talk down to me

GLYNISS: (*Through gritted teeth*) Get out (*He exits*) Right fall in.

(*Clog, Poppy and Patrick enter*)

What have we got? Pat?

PATRICK: I've frozen social media

GLYNISS: Poppy?

POPPY: The vultures have gone; we've got the Met outside

GLYNISS: Excellent work

CLOG: Does anyone want to come in the Hog's Head after work? Few drinks?

GLYNISS: Go back to Hobbiton Frodo, he's not resigning. So this is the situation. As of now we are officially in gridlock

POPPY: The tabloids will be the first to get the full story

GLYNISS: Christ I can see the headlines now "Pig Gate" writes itself. Get the Chief Editors on the blower. Tell them I'm enforcing the mother of all injunctions. If they publicise Pig Gate, I will end their relationship altogether with No. 10. No stories, no scoops, no policies or leaked information, they will be the last to hear, I will give them sweet FA to work under

CLOG: We can't hold them forever

GLYNISS: No, just for the next twelve hours. If this is going public, we're deciding how it's published... So, what's the plan whizz kid?

(*They turn to him. Beat. He thinks*)

PATRICK: We go dark

CLOG: No, terrible idea

POPPY: That certainly looks very weak

GLYNISS: There's no escaping from this, we should just fess up and laugh with everyone

PATRICK: No. The manner in which you react to this could be your defining moment. This will give the people a clear indication of how the Tories deal with idiots, how we will always deal with our enemies. Mature, old fashioned and ruthless

CLOG: Or arrogant, self-righteous and cowardly for not responding

PATRICK: No this will work. We're rising above it. We don't have to respond because it's so childish. We have bigger fish to fry than playground rumours from a bitter ex-MP trying to revive his writing career. If there is nothing to feed the media the story will starve and eventually die

GLYNISS: How does David react when he comes out in daylight?

POPPY: When asked he replies "I'm sure people can see straight through this"

PATRICK: We're not frazzled by silly false claims

POPPY: Lord Ainsworth wrote it purely out of revenge, a personal beef with the PM the media will clearly see

GLYNISS: (*Beat*) Good. That will do. As you were

(*They all exit in different directions. Blackout*)

(*Lights up. 30th April, BCC Studios London, 4.3 million viewers. It's the "Leaders' Presentation Night" a last attempt to win uncertain voters. The Blues enter stage left, the Reds enter stage right. It's going to kick off. Music fades*)

CARTER: Well here we all are, isn't this nice. The Fellowship coming to rescue The Shire accompanied by their obnoxious little troll

NED: How dare you!

WILL: Ned don't, it's not worth it, he's just unloved

CARTER: Sorry I literally have no idea who you are? This your fluffer is it?

WILL: Block yourself from the negativity and enter your safe place (*Ned covers his ears*)

NED: I am the Captain of my own ship

CARTER: Blimey. Hello Shazza, how are you?

SHARON: Hello Dave how's the livestock... still being tampered with?

CARTER: You look good kiddo; all grown up. Oh I see we're still waving the flag on a sinking party whose principles drowned long ago

SHARON: Don't you talk to me about principles you self-obsessed son of a banker! How can you possibly represent the people of Great Britain when you've never missed a meal in your life, never relied on food banks or terrified you might get evicted because the Tories have destroyed social housing? But all these cuts don't matter do they Dave? As long as your business firms are kept happy, you corporate whore!

CARTER: What did you call me you little shit-eating gremlin? (*Removing his blazer*)

SHARON: Oh please you ham-faced animal fucker

CARTER: Careful My Little Pony… careful

SHARON: Oh I will you lanky prick!

(*They square up to one another*)

GLYNISS: Okay stallions let's measure our willies somewhere else shall we?

(*Carter and his gang walk away*)

SHARON: Do it, do it now

NED: No I don't want to

WILL: Ned it's not worth it

SHARON: Go for the fucker

NED: (*Loudly*) Kermit the frog says do you actually love her?!

(*Silence*)

CARTER: (*Turning around slowly*) You what mate?

NED: (*Scared*) I… I

GLYNISS: Right kids calm down, go and play in the street while the grown-ups talk

(*Everyone exits bar Glyniss and Sharon. They meet in the middle, both smile*)

SHARON: Hello Gilly how are you lovely? Long-time no speak

GLYNISS: I'm well Shazz, yourself?

SHARON: Oh well you know… trying to sell Lambrini as Dom Perignon

GLYNISS: Polishing turds has always been our specialty

SHARON: And look at us now

GLYNISS: Remember when we use to braid each other's hair plotting world domination

SHARON: And now we're representing the worst our parties have to offer

GLYNISS: Girl power. Shall we be big girls and talk shop?

SHARON: Yes let's

GLYNISS: What's on the table and what's not?

SHARON: We'd appreciate it if we all avoid Syria

GLYNISS: That's fine, as long as we don't talk about refugees

SHARON: Sure

GLYNISS: With that said, we don't mention what the Yanks or Ruskies are up to

SHARON: And for God's sake let's not get into Europe

GLYNISS: Absolutely, we're still undecided

SHARON: We can mention tax, there's no escaping that, will look odd if we don't

GLYNISS: Well yes naturally. And let's leave the PMS alone shall we?

SHARON: Absolutely, let's not make promises we can't keep. Ned doesn't want to mention Trident or other nations' nuclear disarmament

GLYNISS: Wait, hang on... is he pro nuclear weaponry?

SHARON: It doesn't matter; just lay off it

GLYNISS: Wouldn't we all, right call it (*She tosses a coin*)

SHARON: Heads!

GLYNISS: Tails... sorry petal

SHARON: Thanks Gilly

GLYNISS: Not at all sex bomb, let's coffee soon

SHARON: Of course (*They exit back to their parties*) we're starting

NED: Oh God!

WILL: No this is good. Start well end well

CARTER: (*To Glyniss*) All good?

GLYNISS: Be careful, he's going to go off script, stick to what we rehearsed yes? Let's go over this one last time

(*Both parties give their elective notes, Clog comes forward*)

CLOG: Dave, David, Mr Carter, Prime Minister. Sir, coalition means unity. I am not a device, I am your equal. There is something very wrong with this country… with everything. And we haven't fixed it. We said we would fix it, together. Currently we are living under the Tories, not the coalition. Promises were made. If it wasn't for me, you wouldn't be here (*Carter and Contraband head for their podiums, Clog grabs Carter*)

David I you need to say something

CARTER: (*Scowling*) Get off! (*Carter palms him off*)

WILL: (*Taking Ned aside*) Speak from the heart, truthful honesty

NED: Yes (*He goes to his podium, Sharon grabs him*)

SHARON: Trample and expose him for the rat he is

(*Ned goes to the podium very confused. He starts warming up*)

SHARON: (*Standing in front of him*) And we're going live in Five… four… three… two… one… (*Gestures to go*)

NED: VOICE…! Ladies and gentlemen, in 1974 you silly muppets voted in a fascist female leader known as the "Iron Lady" destroyed this fair land. She sold it to the city boys. But I, Ned Contraband am here to rescue you from further corporate depravity. And I know that you know that I know I can do this. It's. In. Your. Eyes. (*Sharon is not happy*) Things need to change. This coalition is an absolute disaster. (*Sharon gestures more*) Let's face it: it's pretty bleak so far. The PMS is disappearing, Tax is higher than wages and our kids are gonna have a worse life than their parents. Let's create affordable social housing, cut the 1.5 trillion pound debt and balance the books. Let's target the rich by creating a mansion tax, redistribute the wealth and for the love of God let us put working people first. I'll abolish tuition fees in half and stop these obsessive cuts, leaving us with the smallest army on the planet. We're supposed to be out of a recession for Christ sake, so what's that all about... I mean... what a... what a dick (*He laughs*) am I right, am I right?

(*Silence. Sharon gestures for him to get on with it*)

Immigrants are not the issue, they are not stealing our jobs and overpopulating. Nigel Garage is not the answer, he exploits people's fear. The Greens are premature and unrealistic, the Lib Dems are broken, the Tories are lying and the Scottish Nationals want a second referendum. Things need to change, and I promise if you give me your votes, together we will force the Tories out and get Great Britain back again greater back! Thank you! (*He tosses the his papers behind him triumphantly*) Shit!

(*Silence*)

SHARON: And we're out / (*Goes up to Ned*) What was that?

POPPY: And Dave we're on in five... four... three... two... one... go

CARTER: (*Breathes in and out*) People of Britain... at the start of my term I received a letter from the treasury "Dear Chief... there is no money" The last five years have been rebuilding what Labour broke. I had to make incredibly unpopular decisions just to get us back on track. It really is very simple... keep the team that are mending the machine, or... pick the team that broke the machine in the first place. Keep in place the people who actually know where the money is, or elect a leader who is completely dislocated from reality, with his unrealistic promises. Labour say they want to put more money into everything, and when asked how, they simply answer "Tory cuts". Where is the detail, where is the realism, where is the practicality here? I want to make welfare our main priority and get two million people back in work. When kids leave school, there shouldn't be an option of housing benefits and job seeker's allowance. Let them "Earn or Learn", have the opportunity to get an apprenticeship or a place at university. Too many people rely on benefits. We can create jobs and give youngsters hope. I will open five hundred schools, create better and liveable pensions, create harm reduction on drugs and banish child poverty. Let's leave the PMS alone. It's not perfect, so let's keep building it. Listen, military action is the last resort; yet I will not hesitate to use it on ISIS. Nuclear disarmament is a goal we all want to reach, however during these very uncertain times, my main objective is to keep Britain and its allies safe from the terrorist threat, and that is why funding Trident is an imperative (An expensive necessity) but a necessity nonetheless. With regards to coalitions. Nicola Surgeon said she would never form with the Tories. Well let me tell you this... over my dead body will I form a government with the Scottish Nationals. A party who don't even want us to be here. If the British people don't want me in office, I will humbly stand down. If we fall short, I will do the right thing. But I will not cheat myself into office by deceiving voters through a deformed and unwanted government, compromising my programme by bartering away with another party. Unlike the man standing to my left, I have faith and confidence that we can stand alone and get the victory. I will not roll over and let an idiot run this country. I will fight them till the bitter end and they will lose. For I have faith in my programme, my party, and my voters

(*Silence*)

GLYNISS: And... We're... out! Good

(*Both leaders step down from their podiums and their teams gather round, rapidly feeding them information*)

VOICE: Twenty seconds please

SHARON: Right last chance, get up there and leave an everlasting impression you fuck wit

(*Ned goes up to the podium, Will catches him whilst Sharon's back is turned*)

WILL: Sing from the heart, sing from the soul

NED: I will Will (*He turns*)

WILL: Ned?

NED: Yes?

WILL: I love you Ned

NED: I love you too Will

SHARON: And Five… Four… Three… Last chance mate… Two

WILL: From the soul Ned!

SHARON: One… and go!

NED: (*Beat*) So to sum it all up… Stronger economy, higher living standards, PMS good, Immigrants bad… they're not bad! It's complicated. Stop using plastic bags and save the dolphins!

(*Silence. Will gestures "From the Heart"*)

NED: Look… listen… what I'm trying to say is… Everybody's searching for a hero, People need someone to look up to. I never found anyone to fulfil my needs (a lonely place) so I learned to depend on me

(*Silence. Ned knows he's fudged it, Sharon curses*)

POPPY: (*A bit shocked*) Right… so David we're on in five… four… three… make it count… two… one… and go (*Ned is growing with rage*)

CARTER: I pledge to reduce the deficit, create jobs, lower taxes/ tackle

(*Ned steps down from his podium*)

NED: (*With great passion and anger*) I decided long ago not to live in anyone's shadow! If I fail! If I succeed! At least I'll live as I believe. No matter what they take from me. (*Pointing at Carter*) They can't take away my dignity!

(*Silence. Carter doesn't know what to do. Sharon pulls him off the stage*)

(*Silence*)

CARTER: Either let that man run your country. Or leave it to the people who know what they are doing

(*Silence. Ned looks defeated*)

GLYNISS: And… We're… out. Good

(*Silence*)

PATRICK: Now it's up to them

SHARON: Now it's up to them

(*Blackout*)

VOICEOVER: It's ten o'clock, the polls are in, the general election is over now. And our exit poll is predicting the Conservatives are the largest party.

(*Lights up. Whitehall Gardens, post-election party 10:45pm. Ned Contraband is sitting cross-legged on the grass with a champagne bottle. Will remains close whilst Sharon keeps her distance. It's very awkward, nobody knows what to say*)

(*Silence*)

NED: I don't… I don't understand?

WILL: It's not your fault

SHARON: No one could predict this, or the political earthquake in Scotland

NED: They said we were neck and neck?

WILL: A valiant battle

SHARON: Predictions are simply that, we can't take them as anything solid

NED: Did they know this?

SHARON: An inquest into the polling committee has already begun

NED: Twenty two seats… we only gained twenty two seats! I've destroyed the party

WILL: Hey! What's all this now? We all think you did very well

NED: Will… I've lost the election… I've lost the general election you daft prat!

WILL: Well I'm proud of you mate

NED: My political career is over, I'm ruined! All that work… for nothing

WILL: Whatever doesn't kill you makes you stronger

NED: Oh piss off you bloody hippie with your crystal skulls and fortune cookies… this isn't Glastonbury, this isn't Narnia… this is my life's work

SHARON: It's not his fault Ned

NED: And you can fuck off and all… I bet you're loving this?

SHARON: Oi…! You dodged a bullet here, even if by some perverse act of nature you won this election, you would've been torn to shreds by your own party. The House is completely divided! It was a losing battle from the start. No, this is a blessing for you

NED: A blessing…? My life has been torn down because of you two idiots

SHARON: You never had it in you! From the moment you became party Leader I saw a write-off. Listen, you're a good bloke mate but you ain't no leader. You haven't got the panache, the sex, the charisma! (*Beat*) You know this. And I'm sorry to say it, but as much of a posh wanker as he is, Carter fits the bill

(*Silence*)

NED: (*Pitifully*) Did you ever want me to win?

SHARON: ……

NED: Answer the question; did you ever want me to win?

SHARON: I'm not about to compromise everything I stand for to have some spineless worm run this country. A privileged few get that opportunity and you are not one of them. British folk are very good judges of character, and you have been weighed, measured and found wanting

NED: You sabotaged my campaign?

SHARON: You did that yourself

(*Silence*)

NED: (*Takes a deep breath*) Right, where do I go from here?

SHARON: You need a rest

WILL: She's right; your chakras are totally depleted

SHARON: Take a holiday Ned, you need it. You've been slogging your guts out for weeks

NED: You're right I do, I'm exhausted

WILL: The Lake District is very spiritual this time of year

NED: Then I guess I come back and we start again... from scratch. Get a new Cabinet together?

SHARON: Well here's the thing... it doesn't quite work like that

NED: What do you mean?

SHARON: You know what I mean

NED: No I won't let you, I'll regroup, regather! Change my policies/ and start afresh

SHARON: Ned... you don't have a choice. You'll announce your resignation tomorrow

NED: And what if I refuse?

SHARON: You will never set foot in Whitehall again

(*Silence*)

Go back to Doncaster Ned. They'll welcome you like a hero

NED: I don't feel like a hero

WILL: You don't have to be afraid of what you are

NED: (*Furiously*) Don't you dare!

SHARON: Go home to your wife Ned, sit Shiva and grieve. There is more to life than politics

NED: I really don't think there is

SHARON: You're a good man Ned, sorry it wasn't meant to be. Go careful now

(*She exits*)

WILL: She's right… you're a good man

NED: Get. Out

WILL: Mate?

NED: Get out you bloody cretin! Go back to Atlantis or wherever it is you came from

WILL: What about the love Ned?

NED: I never want to see you again, you ruined me!

WILL: What about our hiking trip through Peru?

NED: If I ever see you again I'll have you shot… now get out of here… go on, piss off!

(*With great sadness Will goes to leave. He turns*)

WILL: Always be true to you. Goodbye Ned. I Love you so very much

(*He exits*)

NED: (*On the verge of tears*) I love you too William

(*Ned exits to the bar, Carter enters necking a bottle followed by Clog, who is carrying a large cardboard box with "Liberals" written on it. Clog is protesting passionately*)

CLOG: You swore to me David!

CARTER: Clog, it's over sweetheart

CLOG: Promises were made!

CARTER: Don't be a fool Nick. You sold your soul and you must pay for the consequences

CLOG: You my foul friend did not honour your promises; therefore the contract has been broken!

CARTER: Well the contract is officially now over

CLOG: I sacrificed everything by gambling with you. If it wasn't for me, you wouldn't be here you bloody fascist! This required us to put aside our egos and grab this historic chance for the greater good

CARTER: Oh go cuddle a European you fucking liberal

CLOG: I jumped into bed with you and you didn't even buy me breakfast

(*Glyniss and Patrick enter drinking*)

CARTER: Now let's make one thing perfectly clear. We are here in this situation now because of what my party has achieved, not yours. Yes we did need you, five years ago. And yes we did take advantage of you

CLOG: You're an animal David!

CARTER: Yes. We are all animals. Do not make the catastrophic mistake of thinking you bore any iota of significance whatsoever, you're just the coffee boy. You know I'd have just an ounce of respect for you if you had rejected us, because boy you had some great ideas. What happened to you Nick? But you treat your voters like some five dollar pussy what were you expecting? Now you'll be forever remembered as the Tory sell out who abandoned his promises to swing with the prime-time players. Now piss off back to your depressing solar panelled house in Greenwich, with your eco-friendly hybrid, mongrel rescue cat, and ugly intellectual wife. Don't let the giant black door hit your arse on the way out (*Clog pushes Carter aggressively*)

CLOG: No fuck you Dave... fuck you! Your days are numbered (*He turns to Patrick and Glyniss*) Gilly, you are by far the most foul and disgusting woman I have ever met, and Paddy (*Takes off his tie and hands it to him*) you are the most extraordinary young man, It's been a pleasure of working with you. Save your soul while you still can

(*He exits*)

GLYNISS: Blimey... Nick with testicles, that's new!

PATRICK: This was our doing

GLYNISS: What a colossal waste of life

PATRICK: So it never worked... ever?

GLYNISS: Coalitions are a gross misrepresentation and crime against the British public. No one wants them, yet it's in the rulebook. Well they're bloody gone now; we can rid us of all the bikes clamped outside, whack on the heating and throw out the gays. (*She laughs*) My my David, aren't we a clever boy winning a majority

PATRICK: It was a bit of a close shave

GLYNISS: Nah, we had it in the bag didn't we superstar?

PATRICK: Well done Sir

CARTER: Not at all kiddo, you're pretty handy

GLYNISS: You seem disappointed?

CARTER: It's a strange thing success. What does it matter, I mean what was it all for? Half the people voting make their mind up on the way to the polling station

PATRICK: Surely it's not that bad?

CARTER: It's true, ninety-nine percent of voters buy the image, not the policies. Clog was right, this isn't a democracy, we are all replaceable. (*Turning to Glyniss*) Thank you Gilly, you truly are incredible

GLYNISS: Don't get sentimental on me now

CARTER: I mean it. I would be literally nothing without you (*Beat*) to the next four years eh? (*He walks out*) Cheers Paddy!

(*Exits*)

PATRICK: He's right… no one really cares. All people want is someone with authority who looks like they can hack it and not send this country into oblivion

GLYNISS: It's all terribly reductive isn't it? But that's why we keep going

PATRICK: Is it? Seems pretty bleak!

GLYNISS: It is changing Pat, it really is. I envy your generation and how much better it will all be

PATRICK: Will it? Gilly we might leave Europe

GLYNISS: Come on you're too young to be pessimistic

PATRICK: So we get lacerated tonight and straight back to the grind… shall I prep Dave on the Syria summit?

GLYNISS: (*Beat*) No

PATRICK: Oh really…? Is it already sorted?

GLYNISS: We have someone else dealing with it

PATRICK: But that's my department?

GLYNISS: The thing is Paddy; it's no longer your concern

PATRICK: If I'm being drafted I need to know

GLYNISS: You're not being drafted anywhere… Dave wants you out of No. 10… we're letting you go Pat

PATRICK: I'm sorry?

GLYNISS: On behalf of the Conservative party, the PM would like to thank you for your contribution to the campaign. However we will not be in further need of your skills

PATRICK: Is this a joke?

GLYNISS: Unfortunately not

PATRICK: Do you want this?

GLYNISS: Of course I bloody don't you silly goose, David does

PATRICK: But I practically won him the campaign, those were my strategies

GLYNISS: Yes… I know

PATRICK: I don't believe this, I saved his career!

GLYNISS: What did you expect for God's sake? He is incredibly intimidated by you, everyone is! You are what a leader should be. We're terrified of you, you're brilliant, you're a threat, he has to get rid of you. You were the mastermind of this whole campaign, can't you see how dangerous you are? Listen… you are unbelievably dedicated to the people of this country but you are not a Tory. You're a bloody lefty through and through. You know this (*Beat*) Christ I need a G&T (*She downs her glass*) Look. You will smash it, I promise. Good luck. Keep safe ducky (*She goes to leave*)

PATRICK: Gilly? (*She stops, turns*)

GLYNISS: Yes darling?

PATRICK: (*Beat*) Nothing… It doesn't matter anymore

(*She exits. Patrick stands lost and confused. Ned staggers in, he is drunk and emotional*)

NED: Where is he? I'm gonna bloody kill him!

PATRICK: Ned?

NED: Where's Carter?

PATRICK: What are you still doing here?

NED: I want to challenge him to a dawn at duel

(*Ned collapses on Patrick*)

PATRICK: Sit down for God's sake, here let me get you a glass of water

NED: And a chicken tikka masala with extra naan bread young man

PATRICK: What? I'm not a waiter! Stay here, I'll get you an Uber (*Goes to leave*)

NED: I'm just a floppy floppy sponge

PATRICK: Just hold tight Ned (*He exits, Carter enters behind*)

CARTER: Ah Ned there you are! I need the keys to No. 10. Oh wait… I've already had them for the last five years you silly prick

NED: Dave don't. I'm fragile and emotional

CARTER: Oh you're the fragile one are you? (*Helps Ned get to his feet*)

NED: What are you talking about! You're the king. You're on top the world

CARTER: I'm not Ned. I'm just a twat in a suit with a sell-by date

NED: What happened to us Dave? We're gonna get a second shot aren't we? Tell me it's all gonna be okay?

CARTER: No Ned, you... you fucked up mate. You're done

NED: (*Cries in his chest*) Oh Dave! Where did it all go wrong? How did you do it? What's the secret, tell me?

CARTER: There isn't. I've just got bigger balls

NED: Really?

CARTER: Yeah. I'm just more sellable, that's all it comes down to (*He cries in Carter's arms*) Hey... I've got a season ticket at Peter Stringfellows. How about you and I go get some pussy and cocktails whadya say mate?

NED: No Dave, I can't, I'm married

CARTER: Hey, so am I. We all are. That's why it feel sooooooo good. We're terrible human beings (*Carter dusts off Ned*) Come on, I want to introduce you to Candice and Shaniqua. They're two extraordinary young ladies that are dying to meet you

(*They exit arm in arm, Patrick enters with a glass of water. He goes after Ned and intercepted by the hooded figure*)

PATRICK: Hey wait Ned, come back! (*The hooded figure grabs him*)

CORBZ: You wanted change so badly didn't you?

PATRICK: Sorry who are you?

CORBZ: Yes, who am I indeed? I've been watching you Patrick, all of you, for a very long time

PATRICK: (*Beat*) Jez?

CORBZ: Oh dear Paddy… you have let yourself down. (*He removes his hood*) For I saw a young man with boundless potential but he's lost his way. A man who needs a bit of a kick up the arse to remind him where he's come from, where he's meant to be, and what work is yet to be done

PATRICK: Yes (*Ashamed*) there is something very wrong with this country and we haven't fixed it

CORBZ: Yes there very well is, but we must keep striving for change

PATRICK: But what's the point? Carter's right, no one cares

CORBZ: Tell me right here right now why you, Patrick Houghton, should run this country, what gives you the right and the privilege eh?

PATRICK: (*Beat*) Because I'm a product of this generation/I represent

CORBZ: Oh come off it! How are you different to anyone else that has tried and so miserably failed? What makes you so bloody special?

PATRICK: (*Infuriated*) Because I'm not an over privileged Toff! I'm a human being!

CORBZ: You have a chip on your shoulder

PATRICK: I'm not a minority that represents the majority!

CORBZ: But surely those old Oxbridge boys in their ivory tower can see the plebs below and change everything?

PATRICK: Bullshit! They have no grasp on reality, on the needs of everyday people

CORBZ: But that's not going to change any time soon is it? Ultimately sunshine the posh twats will always rule. In the firms, in the forces, in parliament, all over the world because they have that privilege

PATRICK: Then what's the point then, what's the fucking point? I have no power; there is nothing I can change. It's all corrupt, and it's all tainted and infested. There's no point voting

CORBZ: No boy! No! That's not the answer. So that's what you're going to do Pat... bottle out of it? Abandon politics and work for some internet corporation on 300k a year? Give up on your ancestors who were treated like scum when they emigrated here in the hope of a better quality of life? Don't you dare give up now. If you run away, you just leave them to it. You have been given these gifts, this opportunity, this chance to give back. For what have you given back Patrick? Being a political guru whore to whatever party offers you the most. You know how to play the game, let's play for good reasons

PATRICK: Yes but this country isn't gonna change! Trust me I know, I've been in the Lion's den

CORBZ: You say you know this country, you haven't got a clue. You have an obligation to make it your life's work to commit with every fibre of your being to create a better and equal society. A free national health service to everyone as a human right. Reformed education especially in underprivileged areas, where everyone gets a chance, so in the future there is living proof that you don't have to get into Oxbridge or run around on the playing fields of Eton to excel in life.

PATRICK: Yes...! Yes you're right. The views of young people can't be dismissed as a generation. They are incredibly political, yet they've been put off by us

CORBZ: The fact is politics doesn't care about young people

PATRICK: (*Furiously*) Bullshit, they don't care! And why should they? We have let them down. We live in a society now where more young people know who Kim Kardashian is than what the Holocaust was. Most people don't even bother voting… and to think the suffragettes gave up their lives just for that inch of equality. Our forefathers were slaughtered in the mud hundreds of miles from their loved ones so we wouldn't be slaves to a fascist dictator, yet there's graffiti and White Lightning cans littered on cenotaphs. How can you possibly say the younger generations are switched on? They haven't got a clue of just how lucky they are!

CORBZ: Yes! There it is! There's that fire, that drive to change the unchangeable, enlighten the ignorant, educate the unwilling and help those that are unheard. These are people's lives Patrick. These circus antics must cease, we need to stop playing, stop gambling. Yes I see a young man with boundless potential but he must act! What else?

PATRICK: We must work vigorously for the equal rights of everyone, so it's no longer a projected fantasy but an actual reality and abolish this Tory social cleansing, cap sky-high rents in the capital, re-establish unions in the workplace, stop blaming immigrants for unemployment and the economy. Make homelessness and poverty history

CORBZ: And stop ignoring the colossal problems that are lying on our doorstep. Or have you become such a Tory you've learnt how to ignore the darkest chapters in the catalogue of human history?

PATRICK: Yes, I know, I know! There are refugees camping all over Europe that are being treated worse than dogs in cages! And you're right! We are turning a blind eye to what's on our doorstep. People, families, children that are victims of war that need our help

CORBZ: And at no point is it acceptable in this day and age for countries to use nuclear weaponry as a form of threat to protect itself. We need to disarm, we cannot live in that world. History is there to be learnt from as a brutal reminder of the depths humans can sink. So Patrick... whose side are you on? What are you going to do? Who are you going to do it for?

PATRICK: (*Uncertain*) For the many and not the few?

CORBZ: FOR THE MANY AND NOT THE FEW

(*Corbz disrobes, he's wearing a sequined spandex. The rest of the characters enter and dance their bows. It's weird, cheesy and very unsexy. The End*)